WAKEFIELD
MEMORIES

The publishers would like to thank the following companies for their
support in the production of this book

Asquith Homes

Brotherton Esseco Ltd

Cliff School

The Charlesworth Group

Crofton High School

Gordon's Tyres

E.M.D Parkinson Ltd

Eric France Metals

Harlow & Milner Ltd

H. Hofmann & Sons Ltd

Joseph Rhodes

William Lamb Footwear

Richard Kendall Estate Agents

Silcoates School

Warburtons Bakery

First published in Great Britain by True North Books Limited
England HX3 6AE
01422 344344

ISBN 978 - 1906649098

Text, design and origination by True North Books
Printed and bound by The Charlesworth Group

WAKEFIELD
MEMORIES

CONTENTS

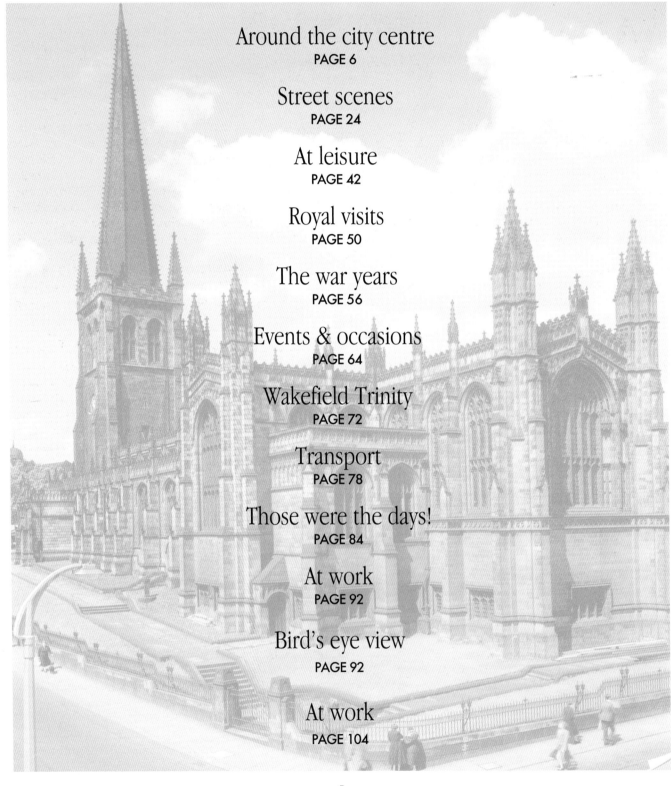

INTRODUCTION

Welcome to 'Wakefield Memories'. This book is the latest in a series that revisits the city our parents and grandparents knew so well. Older readers will recall many of the forgotten scenes for themselves. Younger ones will be able to put in place the sights and sounds of the 20th century Wakefield that they were told about with such affection. This new collection of delightful photographs recalls an era when the pace of life was so different. Once upon a time we had individual and speciality shops. We can see some of them again inside this book. Supermarkets and shopping malls, ugly concrete office blocks and super fast highways were still to come when many of these images were captured. Each one is accompanied by thoughtful captions.

They contain a mixture of fact and reminiscence. All of them are presented with one aim in mind, that of creating a mood of nostalgia for those days that are far behind us. The book makes no apology for indulging in that warm glow of reflecting on the past. Times have changed, not always for the better. However, not everything new is to be dismissed as a lowering of standards. 'Wakefield Memories' will also remind the reader of wartime days, when we feared the worst as bombers flew overhead on missions to the industrial northern heartland of our great nation. Those were the times when food, fuel and clothing were rationed. Thousands went off to fight the enemy and many did not return. There was the depression of the early 1930s and the austere times of postwar Britain. We had few electrical aids in our kitchens and housework was drudgery. We have left those days behind, but they are not forgotten and have to be recalled to gain a balance when we celebrate the happier times.

Within these pages is the opportunity to return to Jackson's the hatter, take a refreshing cuppa in Briggs' café, purchase some pork chops from Zeigler's butchery or hop aboard the tram to Ossett that last ran over 75 years ago. Come back with us to the middle of the century and enjoy the changing face of entertainment. Going to the pictures was replaced by a regular visit to the bingo hall. Crooners such as David Whitfield and Michael Holliday were replaced by rock and rollers. A little box in the corner of the living room brought pictures from the BBC studios right into our homes and we thrilled to share in the Coronation celebrations or that remarkable Matthews' Cup Final between Bolton and Blackpool relayed as outside broadcasts. Before then, we listened to 'ITMA' and Henry Hall on the radio, played card games or amused ourselves with a get together around the piano. Life was more inventive in those days.

The companies and organisations which have developed and thrived in the city over the recent decades are many. We take pleasure in including in this book histories of an outstanding selection of different companies whose contribution to the development and sustainability of the city's economic prosperity is a matter of record. With their co-operation and access to their respective photographic archives, we have been able to tell their stories and hopefully trigger the memories of local people who have worked for them or been touched by their part in community life.

Perhaps the best way to read 'Wakefield Memories' is to get into true period mood. Go to the wardrobe and select an A-line skirt or pair of drainpipe trousers. Put in a set of curlers or slick back your hair with a dab of Brylcreem. Tell the children to close their copies of 'School Friend' and 'Film Fun' and tidy away the Biggles and Famous Five books. As they now annoyingly say in all restaurants, 'Enjoy'.

Image: The original Wakefield coat of arms, used until 1990.

TEXT	ANDREW MITCHELL, STEVE AINSWORTH
PHOTOGRAPH COMPILATION	TONY LAX
DESIGNER	SEAMUS MOLLOY
BUSINESS DEVELOPMENT EDITOR	PETER PREST

AROUND THE CITY CENTRE

Visitors and local inhabitants alike cannot fail to be impressed by the changes that have overtaken our city in the years since the start of the new millennium. These changes are continuing still as this vibrant place keeps pace with the needs and aspirations of an ever developing society. It may be that, in years to come, not every initiative will be seen as having born fruit, but at least it will not be for the lack of trying. Of course, this means that the face of the place we love has to alter to meet fresh challenges, just as it has done for decades and centuries before. Wakefield refuses to stand still and be a fuddy duddy as it meets the demands of the 21st century head on.

The balance between modernisation and heritage is a difficult one to get right, but the more attention that our planners give to marrying the two harmoniously then the better it will be for reactionaries and revolutionaries alike. Looking around the centre, we know that key retail and commercial areas were redeveloped in the immediate postwar years. This process was repeated at the start of the 1980s and, as we turn to look at the area again at the present time, it shows just how adaptable and forward thinking Wakefield folk can be. It is perhaps only now that we can start to think that we have just about recovered from the collapse of the mining industry that crippled the county's villages and communities that relied on the fossil fuel for their existence. Naturally, it has not all been plain sailing and things have been further hampered by the recession that first hit hard in late 2008. But, Yorkshire folk are made of stern stuff and there is a determination in the air not to be beaten down by external factors. We are Tykes after all.

The photographs in this section show how our city centre has altered its look in the same way that a woman who is fashion conscious does her hair, adjusts her hemline or adapts her make up to suit the passage of time. Keen observers will note the similarity between bright, light and airy clothing and styles that are mirrored in the design of modern buildings and point out that a darker, more sombre dress sense seemed to suit the building fashions of earlier times.

Above: Motor buses first appeared on the streets of Wakefield in 1922. The single decker variety seen here on a wintry day in Cross Square was one of the first to be introduced. It heralded the demise of the tram that would be completed within a decade.

CROSS SQUARE

Left: In 1969 councillors walked along Cross Square as part of the overture to the formal induction service to be conducted in the Cathedral welcoming the new Provost. As All Saints still acted as a parish church, the head of the Cathedral Chapter was called Provost and not Dean.

Right: The 1950s was a decade of rebuilding both property and lives. The postwar years were difficult as we struggled to get back on our feet and live a life of normality once more. Days like this on Cross Square were ones we wanted; days filled with sunshine and promise.

Others will point out that the up-to-date shops and office blocks have little to offer in terms of heritage and fine detail, being the equivalent of the throwaway carton in our fast food society. Differences of opinion, but opinion nonetheless.

What cannot be argued is the debt we owe to our forebears. They founded and shaped the city we have grown to love, warts and all as Cromwell put it. It is thought that there was little in the way of settlement here until the Angles came up the River Calder about 1,500 years ago. The current name of our city possibly developed from the Anglo Saxon term Wacanfeld, namely the field belonging to a certain Waca. However, others put forward the theory that it is named for a field where a watch was kept or a wake was held. In the 9th century, the Vikings held sway and some of the names here can be traced back to that tribe of folk notorious for pillaging and other unmentionable activities. The 'gate' part of Northgate, Westgate and Kirkgate meant nothing to do with a point of entry, but was simply the word the Vikings used for 'road'.

The tram heading along Kirkgate, in the direction of the Six Chimneys public house, was in the vicinity of what became a large roundabout at the end of Marsh Way. There has been more what the authorities call 'remodelling' near here in recent times.

Centre: A fine drop of Samuel Smith's Tadcaster Ale awaited drinkers at the Double Six on Kirkgate. The pub's name reminds us of the days when games such as dominoes, fives and threes, crib, nap, don and solo whist were commonplace in the smokey tap room.

Looking from the Six Chimneys towards Warrengate in late Victorian times showed busy pavements, but little in the way of vehicles on the street. How that would change in years to come as electric trams, motor cars and buses soon dominated the highways and byways.

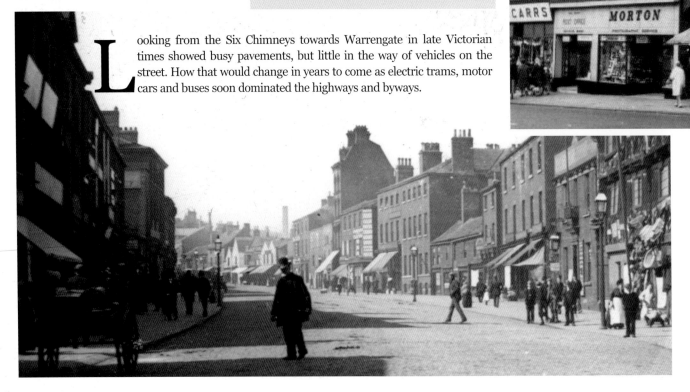

KIRKGATE

Below: *Marks & Spencer on Upper Kirkgate was doing good business in the early 1960s. Next door, Weaver to Wearer described itself as 'tailors to the modern world'. Other similar retailers also had special slogans they used to advertise their wares, Burton's was 'the tailor of taste' and John Collier had 'the window to watch'.*

Left: *The southern end of Kirkgate was widened after the last war and many familiar buildings were demolished, including The Beehive, a favourite watering hole. Burton's, on the left, was one of the many facades that owed much to the 1930s' vogue for art deco.*

NORTHGATE

Settlements were established in this vicinity and the first church built was a modest wooden building dedicated to All Hallows.

Sadly, despite becoming a well to do place, the town fell foul of William the Conqueror's 'harrying of the north' campaign when the new king laid waste to large tracts of the region. This was part of a scorched earth policy designed to suppress northern rebels after the Norman Conquest. Even so, we were mentioned in the Domesday Book 20 years later as 'Wachfeld'.

This was a town that would not die. Despite the treatment meted out by William I. Wakefield rose again. In the early 13th century, King John granted us the right to hold an annual fair. A further charter, drawn up by Henry III in 1258, extended the number of occasions on which fairs could be held. These, along with the weekly markets, helped bring both people and prosperity to the area. The market was sited in the vicinity of what became the Bull Ring and many of the stalls were later converted into housing on Little Westgate, Bread Street, Butcher Row and Silver Street. Further wealth came to the town during this medieval period thanks to our position on the river. Wakefield became an important inland port, with major interests in the woollen trade, tanning and cattle dealing. Coal was being mined and this would later become an influential commodity.

The town was touched by two major internal English wars. The Battle of Wakefield took place in 1460, during the War of the Roses. The Duke of York and his son, the Earl of Rutland, were both killed not far from Sandal Castle and thousands of Yorkists were butchered or confined in the Tower of London. It is thought that the nursery rhyme, 'The Grand Old duke of York' dates from this time. Two centuries later Parliamentarians captured the town from the Royalists during the English Civil War, but more settled times lay ahead.

Bottom: *Horse buses, similar to this one on Northgate in 1890, were the first forms of local public transport to be seen on our roads. However, their shortcomings in distance travelled and the number of passengers carried meant that they were of limited value. For a while there was a flirtation with horse drawn and steam powered trams, but it was the use of electricity that was to change everything.*

Right: *You might have expected a pop star, such as Jimmy Young or Alma Cogan, to preside at the opening of a new Northgate shop. Instead, it was the Mayor who did the honours with scissors and ribbon at Noel Fashions on 25 November, 1956.*

By about 1960, the Northgate junction at Kingswell's Corner, with its row of fine Georgian buildings, was heavy with the traffic that would blight all our city centres in the years to come, as bumper to bumper became the norm.

Right: Pictured in 1965, the new shops on redeveloped The Springs are typical of the period. Architects went in for rectangular shapes and boring lines. Individuality was replaced by practicality. Contrast that with the delights of the Triumph Herald parked up here. Manufactured in a variety of bright colours, it had a style that poked out its tongue at conformity.

Shopping came to a halt at Wakefield Market on 16 June 1961. On the corner of Teall Street with The Springs, canny shoppers sought out the best of bargains before stallholders closed to allow redevelopment to begin.

THE SPRINGS

The Springs provides a pleasant approach to the Cathedral Church of All Saints that stands on the site of a former Saxon church. In 1992 it became only the second British cathedral to boast a girls' choir.

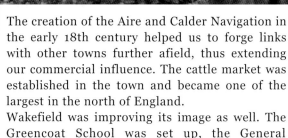

The creation of the Aire and Calder Navigation in the early 18th century helped us to forge links with other towns further afield, thus extending our commercial influence. The cattle market was established in the town and became one of the largest in the north of England.

Wakefield was improving its image as well. The Greencoat School was set up, the General Dispensary established, streets paved and lit by oil lamps, turnpikes constructed and the town's population doubled to 8,000 in the century leading up to the start of the industrial revolution. Wakefield was now at the height of its material prosperity as a trading centre for both raw materials and finished cloths. Families such as Milnes, Heywood and Naylor were nicknamed 'The merchant princes'. They built large houses in Westgate to demonstrate their power and wealth. The town was still centred on the parish church, with the surrounding streets being crammed with a mixture of shops, houses and small workshops. With the increase in industrialisation and the rapid rise in population during the first half of the 19th century, the housing in the centre became overcrowded and insanitary. Wakefield began to spread out, encompassing Eastmoor, Primrose Hill and Belle Vue where houses were built for those seeking work in the new grain mills, maltings, iron foundries, chemical works and textile spinning mills. New coal mines were sunk on the town's outskirts, with some 46 in operation by the time that Queen Victoria had celebrated her silver jubilee. However, it was not all grime and smoke. Wakefield was part of the Rhubarb Triangle, along with Morley and Rothwell, and this crop flourished thanks to the right combination of soil, rainfall, soot and cheap heating fuel to promote the growth of forced rhubarb.

By the start of the last century, major developments in our way of life were in their infancy or soon to be with us. These would affect the very nature of the town and city centres up and down the country. Wakefield was no exception. The noted architect, George Gilbert Scott, had directed the restoration of the parish church, following which it was reconsecrated as a cathedral in 1888 in line with the new city status that had been granted. This reflected Wakefield's increasing dominance as the main town in the area as well as being the administrative centre of the West Riding, though Leeds would soon challenge this. The population of

Above: *The buildings to the left that stood on Westgate in the early 1900s have since given way to a car park. There was no need for these a century ago when shoppers had time to stroll and chat without feeling the pressure of the clock ticking as wardens waited to pounce on motorists who overstayed their welcome.*

23,000, though this figure can be multiplied many times when including the suburbs, enjoyed the introduction of electrification in public transport with the age of the new tram system starting in 1904.

WESTGATE

Where Westgate now bustles with shoppers moving freely along its pedestrianised areas, there was once a busy thoroughfare. Seen towards the end of the Edwardian era, the open topped tram was a modern marvel of the day, helping to revolutionise local public transport. The passengers were in for a draughty journey to Agbrigg.

The first motor cars drove along the road and an occasional aeroplane was seen in the sky above Westmorland Street before the outbreak of the Great War. Ladies took to the streets demanding parity in the polling booth and we moved from the Victorian era to the Edwardian age.

After that war we expected that our boys would return to homes fit for heroes, as the government had promised, but who believes in anything any government says, whether then or now? During the 1920s, some efforts were made to fulfil the pledges and new estates at Portobello, Lupset and Eastmoor were built. But even this did not fully replace the level of substandard housing that still existed. By the 1930s, Wood Street and Westgate had men standing around on corners with nothing to do as the unemployment figures spiralled upwards. Those were tough times, with little in the way of state funding to support the jobless and deprived.

WESTMORLAND STREET

Left: Taken on 2 August, 1939, this was Westmorland Street just as demolition work was about to begin on a number of the properties we see here. It seems incongruous now, as just a month later war was declared on Germany. Some cynics suggested that putting a large cross on the roofs would have saved taxpayers money as the Luftwaffe could have done the job for us.

Above: The Bull Ring and Westmorland Street in the early 1960s was part of the hub of the city. Its importance was underlined when a major refurbishment programme was begun in late 2008. It is expected that the various phases of improvements will take at least five years to complete.

Left: The elevated view of the Westmorland Street shops was taken in the 1950s. The vista beyond the sweep of the retail outlets in the foreground shows just how built-up and congested a place Wakefield has become.

WOOD STREET

Right: *Acting as Wakefield Museum since 1955, this squat edifice on Wood Street was built in 1821-23 with a music saloon, newsroom, bank, cellar baths and public dispensary. In 1855 it became the Mechanics' Institute and in 1910 was transformed into the Institute of Literature and Science.*

Right inset: *The Museum, on Wood Street, photographed in the 1970s, is in the foreground, with other municipal buildings beyond. They include the Town Hall, Crown Court and County Hall among others. The grandeur and elegance of these buildings are appropriate to their purpose.*

Top right: *Looking up Wood Street from the general direction of the Bull Ring not long after World War I, the bobby on traffic duties was a recent addition to the streets of Britain. He was glad to return to other tasks when electrically controlled lights were introduced, but they did not become commonplace until the 1930s.*

Bottom right: *The austerity 50s were giving way to the swinging 60s when this scene was captured along Wood Street, looking north from the junction with Silver Street and Bull Ring. The private motor car became a commonplace family possession in this era.*

We lived through another world war, with bomber aircraft overhead and our brave boys off to die on a foreign field, just like their fathers before them. At least we were spared the sort of aerial hammering that was given to the likes of Leeds, Bradford and Sheffield. Postwar austerity meant that rationing and shortages continued, but we got the NHS, a properly organised education service and the welfare state, so some things really did get better. By the time that Macmillan reminded us in the late 1950s that we had 'never had it so good', there were ordinary people driving cars along Westgate, televisions in most living rooms and very few queuing at the Labour Exchange. Fridges and washing machines became commonplace in the 1960s and homes were built with central heating as standard. As Bob Dylan put it, 'The times they were a-changing'. We could see that for ourselves with the high rise flats just off George Street and on Kirkgate. There was the new Brook Street Market and, later, the Ridings Shopping Centre. As we prepare for more changes and makeovers in the city centre, wallow for a while in the nostalgia induced by these photographs of times gone by.

COUNTY HALL

ounty Hall is now the main headquarters of Wakefield City Council. Standing on the corner of Bond Street and Cliff Parade, it was built in 1894-98 on the site of Rishworth House, the gentleman's house that had once been owned by Thomas Rishworth Snr. It originally served as the administrative centre for the West Riding County Council until this was redefined in the local government reorganisation of 1974. The original opening ceremony was a very formal and serious affair, as can be seen by the top hats and frock coats that were worn. The West Riding was formed by the Local Government Act of 1888 and a first meeting held in Wakefield Town Hall the following year. Competition between Wakefield and Leeds for the honour of hosting the Council's permanent home was resolved in our favour in 1892. James S Gibson was commissioned to draw up the design. He was well known as a winner

of design competitions and would later be remembered for the stylish Middlesex Guildhall. Armitage and Hodgson won the building contract and County Hall took shape, culminating in this ceremony that was conducted on 22 February 1898. The Marquess of Ripon was the presiding dignitary. His claim to fame was that he had been born at 10 Downing Street, London. He was the son of FJ Robinson, 1st Viscount Goderich, who served as Prime Minister for just a few months in the late 1820s.

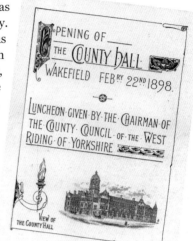

Thomas Rishworth was formerly a partner in the Townend and Rishworth Bank. His business acumen made him a

Above: Rishworth House in the early 1890s. Right: The opening ceremony of the new County Hall in 1898. Above right: A luncheon menu from the opening ceremony.

wealthy man, rich enough to be able to afford to build Rishworth House on Bond Street. By 1826 Rishworth had amassed a personal fortune which by today's reckoning would have made him a multi-millionaire. He had already built this house for his first born son, also Thomas, who had been made a partner in the bank. Thomas Snr continued to live at Birthwaite Hall, near Darton. He was a highly-regarded man who held distinguished office, being Chief Constable of Wakefield, serving on the Poor Relief and Watch Committees and being a governor of Wakefield Grammar School. As rapid as had been the rise to riches, so the descent to rags was just as swift. The bank collapsed and Thomas was made bankrupt. He had to sell Birthwaite Hall and he returned to Hemsworth where he died in 1843. Several of his children ended up as beggars or in the workhouse, while others started life again in Australia. Ownership of Rishworth House passed to West Riding Quarter Sessions. It was demolished in the 1890s, not long after this photograph was taken.

Left: The County Hall pictured shortly after completion. Below: Alderman T Tomlinson welcomes Princess Elizabeth to County Hall in 1949.

MARKET HALL

Above: Pictured towards the end of the 19th century, Wakefield Market Hall was well established as the major shopping centre of its day. A small funfair, with swingboats and stalls, had been set up alongside the building. This was a reminder of former times when open markets were held and they attracted more than just stallholders. The crowds who came to shop would also be entertained by travelling troubadours, street actors, jugglers, stilt walkers and fire eaters. They were also places where more unpleasant activities were practised. Pickpockets found easy pickings in the jostling throngs and conmen enjoyed fleecing the naïve with their three card tricks or sale of life enhancing potions that were merely coloured water. The Lord of the Manor, Earl Warren, gained royal permission from King John to hold the first ever market in the town in 1204. It was held over a three day

Left: As is typical of nearly all buildings from this decade, concrete abounded. Where once there was handsome stone, now there was an amorphous mass of grey cement, aggregate and water. Such was progress in the swinging 60s. This new build cost £289,000 and offered 87 stallholders a site from which to trade, along with separate fish and meat stalls. The market was erected on the site of the old one that had served shoppers for well over a century. While the replacement was taking shape, trading took place in the open air and some of these outdoor stalls were retained even after the new market was brought into use. Yet another new market opened in 2008 at a cost of £3 million. The controversial design by David Adjaye divided public opinion. Traditionalists trembled with trepidation when they heard the architect describe his plans with the words, 'Buildings are deeply emotive structures which form our psyche.' Funny, that. We always thought that they were places in which to work, rest or play.

Below: When the Market Hall opened in 1963, it was popular with a new breed of shoppers. They had aspirations beyond those held by their parents. Mum and dad were content to live their lives having enough to pay the rentman, keep the wolf from the door and enjoy a couple of weeks in Cleethorpes every summer. The wind of change was not just blowing across South Africa, but down Britain's High Streets and housing estates as well. In Pretoria it was apartheid that was to be challenged, but at home it was the old order and lifestyle that was under threat. Shoppers demanded more varied produce from the food stalls and brighter, younger clothes from the department stores. They demanded all the mod cons of domestic life. Young couples looked to purchase their own property away from the council estates and terraced back to backs of their childhood. They intended to fill them with TVs, washing machines, fridges and tumble driers. There was to be a family saloon on the drive and a holiday in Brittany or one of the Costas. Consumerism arrived long before Mrs Thatcher was a power in the land. Young women moved around the Market Hall looking for the ingredients to make their very own prawn cocktail as a starter for the dinner party they were holding for friends from the office this coming Saturday. A bottle of Mateus Rose or Hirondelle would make a fine accompaniment.

period. Pressure from traders anxious to sell their goods in more comfortable surroundings led to the building of the Victorian Market Hall. Permission for the building work to take place was granted in 1847 and completed by 29 August 1851. It was to serve us well until the demolition ball swung its way in 1962.

Bottom left: An intense discussion seems to be taking place in the marketplace in this photograph that dates from the turn into the 20th century. Perhaps they were discussing the war in South Africa where the Boers were making merry at the expense of our boys who seemed a little out of their depth in that particular conflict. At home we celebrated the diamond jubilee of the grand old royal, Queen Victoria, when, in 1897, she reached the landmark of 60 years as our monarch. She was still with us as the new century dawned. Perhaps those pictured talked about items they could buy in the market. The choice in the photograph lay between potted plants and wallpaper, but if they ventured inside the hall there was much more on offer. At that time, there were 28 indoor stalls offering a variety of meats, confectionery, dairy products, millinery, ironmongery and books. The open air stalls held fruit, vegetables, fish, clothing, china and tobacco. There was even a blacksmith in attendance. The old Market Hall was typical of buildings that lasted for many more years than their replacements. Not only do concrete, steel and glass die more quickly, they linger in the memory for a much shorter time as well.

STREET SCENES

Below: The owners of the horse cabs were not happy with the march of progress. The introduction of tramlines through the Bull Ring and out towards the suburbs was going to affect their business quite dramatically. Gardeners were far from thrilled with the prospect as roses and rhubarb did not respond as well to droppings left by trams. Buckets full of steaming manure made men with green fingers very happy, though it must be admitted that the roads in city centres in our country were often quite smelly and unattractive places as allotment holders did not keep pace with the volume deposited on the cobbles. In the early 1900s, the gentle pace of life was soon to be challenged. For most people, Shanks's pony or the real thing was used to get about on short journeys. They thought little of walking a few miles into a town or village centre before making their way back home again, shopping crooked over their arms. Workers covered the same distance heading off to work and

children happily skipped along, following a well trodden route to the classroom. Railways helped some commute, but this form of transport was often reserved for longer journeys. As the century unveiled, the power of electricity unleashed the tram and the development of the petrol engine heralded another new way of getting about. The horses continued to bury their heads in their nosebags on the Bull Ring for several more years, but it was not long before the lucky ones were turned out into fields. A more desperate fate at the glue factory or pet food store awaited the others.

Above: The memorial to Queen Victoria was unveiled on 15 February 1905 when traffic was much lighter. The police became very concerned about congestion in the 1920s and took this photograph to make a point to the council that measures had to be taken to ease the flow around the city centre. Vehicles were clogging the roads, creating traffic jams, causing hazards for pedestrians and polluting the air with their fumes. How often have we heard all that over and over again as decade after decade has gone by? It just goes to show that there's nowt we have not heard before. The half a dozen motor taxis waiting to ply their trade from their base in the centre of the Bull Ring were a fairly new addition to city centre life. They would be used by the middle classes who did not want to sully themselves by travelling on a common tram with working class types who might be carrying germs and the like or were just too far beneath them in social standing to be tolerated as fellow passengers. The taxi has become, in more modern times, the conveyance of the young. Those of us brought up in the austere 1950s wince at the thought of paying someone to take us into town, but today's youngsters think nothing of it.

Above: It was not so much trouble at t'mill, but problems with the coal mines in the early 20th century. Although improvements had been made to the working conditions in the mines, children no longer went underground and safety records were better than they once were, the employers still ruled the roost. Their main consideration was profit and this was the driving force behind any action or decision. Control was exercised over the workforce by a refusal to accept the existence of trade unions and a denial that miners had much in the way of rights. The colliery owners were supported in law in the early 1800s and miners attempting to form a union found themselves in hot water with the authorities. In 1834, farmworkers from Tolpuddle in Dorset tried to circumnavigate the Combinations Act by forming a Friendly Society, but they were prosecuted for 'swearing oaths' and transported to Australia. In 1889, Ben Pickard, a Yorkshire miner, decided to form the Miners' Federation along with some others, including James Keir Hardie. The bosses continued to resist any demands from their workers as best they could. They also owned many of the homes in which the mining families lived, so exercising further control. The major dispute over pay saw sanctions being imposed by wholesale evictions, as witnessed at Kinsley. On 3 October 1905, one of the last of the homes to be emptied was photographed as a policeman pushed a mangle out through the door and another lowered a bed from a first floor window.

Below left: The police have never been popular with the mining community as they were seen as agents of the government and the colliery owners when the mines were privately owned. In April 1904, the Hemsworth Fitzwilliam Collieries Company decided to apply swingeing pay cuts to miners working on two of their three coal seams. Some men immediately went on strike, leading to a long-lasting and increasingly bitter conflict. By the summer of 1905, seams were closed down, pay cut and surface workers sacked. The eviction of families from their colliery-owned homes began in earnest. The police were called in to keep the peace and see that the process was carried out with the minimum of fuss. Here, three bobbies helped by rolling up bedding for one family, but the boys in blue were regarded with suspicion and called such names as 'employers' lackeys' and worse. Not surprisingly, the police responded by being heavy handed in the way they handled a lot of the property in the houses. The miners and their loved ones had to move out into tents and rooms where friends and wellwishers provided assistance. The landlord of the Kinsley Hotel turned his ballroom into a dormitory that children could use. However, many miners were still without homes and jobs over a year later. These were truly difficult times for ordinary folk.

Above: Hallelujah! Salvation is nigh. Well, in actual fact it had arrived in Ossett on 6 August, 1909, in the form of the blood and fire man himself, the self-styled General William Booth (1829-1912). Founder of the Salvation Army, or 'Sally Army' as most of us affectionately called it, he was carried in one of two rather swish open tourers that swept along Church Street, near the junction with Dale Street, in front of an interested knot of onlookers. They stood outside a small café and we can just about make out adverts for Lipton's Tea and Fry's Chocolate on the shop frontage. Booth had passed through Chickenley Heath and was on his way to a reception at the Town Hall. He was a former Methodist lay preacher. As a child, he was well educated until his schooling came to a sudden halt when his formerly wealthy father was suddenly bankrupted. As a young man he preached to the 'poor and sinners' of Nottingham, his home town. He moved to London and founded his Christian Mission in 1875 and transformed this into the Salvation Army in 1878. Attitudes towards the Army softened as years went by and heaven help anyone in even the roughest of public bars who swore at or was rude to a lass in a Sally Army uniform who came into the pub selling the 'War Cry'.

Below: The imposing building of the Grand Clothing Hall completely dominated the Bull Ring and Cross Square towards the end of the first decade of the last century. Edwardian England lasted less than 10 years, a short span when compared with over 60 years of the Victorian era and the similar period to come with the second Elizabethan age. Yet, during the comparatively brief reign of Edward VII, there was a certain style to the time and it had its own moments that were peculiarly Edwardian. The class system was very rigid, but the movement towards women's suffrage gathered momentum. The period had its own architectural style, fashion, way of life and art nouveau was prominent. In towns, trams dominated public transport and, overhead, aeroplanes first took to the skies. With an increasingly literate population, mass audience newspapers became more important. Major literary figures, such as Galsworthy, Wells, Bennett, Forster and Conrad were in their prime and the phonograph brought Caruso into our homes. The first movie houses were built and the Olympic Games came to London. The Grand Clothing Hall was built in 1906 and served the city as a major outfitter for many years. It is now a Grade II listed building, home to a variety of retail outlets.

Right: The drinking fountain and horse trough that was donated to Ossett in the 1891 will of Hannah Pickard was erected two years after the death of the benefactor. She also made bequests and gave monies to support local hospitals, the grammar school and several churches and chapels. The Market Place memorial to her provided the backdrop for this large group from Dale Street Mission, photographed in 1911. Dale Street United Methodist Church, sometimes called the place of the Wesleyan Reformers, was built in 1857. There was a national dedication to organised religion 150 years ago and Christianity was represented in a variety of different codes that include the straightforward RC and C of E, along with Methodists, Wesleyans, Congregationalists, Baptists and Zionists. Eleven churches and chapels were built in and around the town in a 10 year period in the middle of the 19th century. Splinter groups continually broke away and founded their own branch of

Christianity and, at times, their own branch of a branch. In 1895, the United Methodist Chapel was opened on Dale Street. This building later became a gym. The local Mission Hall was a form of religious community centre and was often used to encourage children to get involved with formalised religion at an introductory level.

Bottom right: The Queens Hotel, Tanshelf, in Pontefract opened in 1901 as the main one serving passengers using the nearby railway. The high ceilings, large windows and distinctive façade and turreted roof make the building a most impressive sight as you drive along Front Street. In days gone by, the surrounding location was not as built up as it is today. Guests found the experience of staying at The Queens a most relaxing and charming one. In the 1930s, it was one of the places to be when in

Pontefract. The two chaps standing by one of the cars adopted quite a raffish pose. Maybe they were the Hooray Henrys of their era. For them life could have been one of anyone for tennis, strawberries and cream and croquet on the lawn. Is there honey still for tea? During the interwar years. Britain was still split into a have and have-not society. Millions were out of work and families struggled to get by on a daily basis. For them, this was the 'Love on the dole' about which Walter Greenwood wrote. Our pictured group was more used to the world of 'Rebecca' and Manderley, as created by Daphne du Maurier.

Right: The opening of a new bridge was something that seems to have captured the interest of large numbers of locals. They flooded across it in their hundreds, with many more lining the way as an official procession with VIPs aboard a motorcade passed by. This took place on 1 June 1933, Wakefield's 'Year of Progress' as it had been designated by those trying to breathe some life into a struggling local economy. The old Chantry Chapel Bridge was replaced as the main access point to the route south to Barnsley and Doncaster across the River Calder when the new one

opened alongside it. Named because priests used to chant dirges for lost souls, a chantry located on a bridge was not unusual in bygone times. It was sited there to provide easy access for travellers wishing to say a quiet prayer or enjoy a period of quiet reflection. They gave thanks for safe arrival in a town and asked for further protection on the next leg of their journey. Today, there are only six such chantries still in use. Wakefield's Chantry Chapel of St Mary the Virgin is the only surviving one of four that once ringed the city. They stood at the main entrances to the medieval town at Westgate, Northgate, Eastmoor and here. St Mary's was licensed in 1356 and a toll was levied on travellers crossing the river at this point.

Bottom left: Originally Ossett-cum-Gawthorpe when formed in 1866, the town became simply Ossett in 1890. Its roots go much further back than the latter years of the 19th century as mention is made in the Domesday Book of Osleset, a hamlet in the Manor of Wakefield. When it was created a municipal borough, the plan was for the town to be part of Kirklees. After a number of protests that Huddersfield as a centre was too remote, Ossett became allied with Wakefield. It relied for its prosperity at the time on a large number of small textile mills and coal mines. It had brief fame as a spa town and it

was hoped that it might emulate Harrogate, but little came of the idea. Its only links with international recognition are now dependent on the world coal carrying championship held each Easter Monday at Gawthorpe and that Black Lace, the pop duo of 'Agadoo' renown, hail from Ossett! This was Market Place with Bank Street in 1953, as seen from the Town Hall. The Midland Bank is the large building on the right, opposite Hagenbach's bakery, C.M. Paul's clothes shop and the Clock and Bottle public house. The bus on the left standing by the phone boxes and public toilets is alongside the Hannah Pickard Memorial Fountain that was donated to the town in 1893 by a local family of mill owners. When Market Place was redeveloped, the fountain was moved to Green Park, but only a portion of it remains standing.

Below: For a moment it might appear that Burton, the tailor of taste, had turned its hand to another meaning of the word. The fresh fish stall, though, was nothing to do with the famous store that continues to trade under this name today. There was a fine variety of seafood to be had on the stall and, according to the promotional banner, it was all freshly caught and supplied direct to the counter. It was obviously a popular stall, to tell from the queue that had built up. Of course, fresh fish is especially attractive to the palate. Frozen fish fingers and prepared stuff hidden away in cardboard boxes or behind plastic wrapping is just not the same. Our predecessors could actually taste the sea when they bit into a nice piece of cod or snapped open a shell to retrieve a tasty morsel of crabmeat.

Above: Typical. You work your socks off for weeks on end, knowing that August Bank Holiday is just around the corner and what does it do when the day actually dawns? It chucks it down. We should have known better than make plans for a nice day out in the countryside or to join in with friends on a 'charrer' ride to Mablethorpe. There is something perverse about the British weather in that it seems to know just when to turn nasty at the most inconvenient time. You could almost guarantee that the heavens would open when the Aussies were about to play a Test match at Headingley and so it was on 7 August 1922 when the day was spoiled by the rain that hammered down. We did not have that many Bank Holidays, so it was all the more annoying to have this one ruined. Until 1834, the Bank of England observed 33 saints' days as holidays, but these were not public ones and workers outside the banking industry gained no benefit from them. The formal arrangements were put in place by Sir John Lubbock, who introduced the Bank Holidays Act in 1971. Good Friday and Christmas Day were already regarded as public holidays, but he saw to it that Easter Monday, Whit Monday, the first Monday in August and Boxing Day were acknowledged. People were so grateful for a paid break, albeit a brief one, that the holidays were called 'Lubbock's Days' for a while. Many flocked to the coast on specially arranged trains, helping the resorts to enjoy increased profits. August Bank Holiday was moved to the end of the month in 1965. These people seen on Westgate End wished the move had come much earlier. Then they might have avoided a very damp holiday. Left of centre, the stream on Westgate is nearly lapping over the top of the wall. The terraces on the left belonged to Morton Parade and Plumpton Parade.

Top right: Perhaps this photograph from the late 1940s inspired the American singer Jane Morga to record 'The day that the rains came down' a decade later. It was to top the British singles' charts in early 1959 and it was her only major hit record. She stayed in this country for a while on the back of that record's success and even tried to represent us in the Eurovision Song Contest, but Pearl Carr and Teddy Johnson were selected instead. The floods on Denby Dale Road did not seem to deter the couple in the foreground from having a bit of fun. The old chap behind them seems to be saying, 'Knees up, Mother Brown', but the woman didn't need any encouragement in letting her hair down and her skirts up.

Below: Lime Pit Lane is a residential street in Stanley, not far from the River Calder and the Aire and Calder Navigation. Just after the last war, someone in the street was about to move house. Queen's Transport, a local firm that specialised in furniture removals, had been commissioned to attend to the job of shifting all the furniture and chattels to a new home. But the van was almost marooned in the middle of the street. It made its way gingerly forward as two removal men gazed forlornly out of the rear doors. Just how they were going to get the job done without a lot of problems was anyone's guess. The thought of lugging a bulky wardrobe down the front garden path, ankle deep in water, with sheets covering it to protect the wood from the elements was going to be some task. The struggle through the floodwater and the extra work entailed meant that time was going to be added to the day. The men had only negotiated a set fee for the job, so they would be working for less money per hour the longer the move took. No wonder there were glum expressions on their faces. The householder had better put the kettle on as they would need an endless supply of tea to keep their spirits up.

Right: The Virgin Queen was on the throne when the Six Chimneys was built and the façade retained much of that Elizabethan style throughout its life. The date 1566 was carved above the door and on the gable end, so it had been here for about 350 years when this snapshot was taken. At this time, the ground floor was home to a couple of shops. T. Thompson sold furniture and P. Bell was a basket maker. Inside, a massive 16-feet-wide chimney channelled the fumes from various fireplaces out into the open air via the six flues and chimney pots on the roof. Only wealthy families

could afford such large houses and well engineered smoke removal systems in Tudor times, so the people who initially owned this house had more than a groat or two in the pockets of their doublet and hose. Finely carved panelling and mighty oak staircases added to the opulence of the Six Chimneys that was one of the most distinctive edifices ever to grace Kirkgate. Carelessly carried out internal repairs and the removal of a supporting wall caused the collapse of the building in 1941. The Tetley's pub to the left was the Crown and Anchor. Just further along Kirkgate, there is a Six Chimneys pub that is part of the J D Wetherspoon group. It opened there in 1999, though the façade hardly compares with the classy style of the original.

Below left: This photograph dates from a time during the blitz on Britain when the German Luftwaffe launched its deadly attacks on our cities during World War II, and at first sight this would appear to be the aftermath of an air raid. However, it was no such thing. The hackneyed phrase, 'it looks like a bomb has just hit', was apt but inaccurate. The Six Chimneys underwent some internal alterations during the spring of 1941, but at 7.45 on the evening of 16 May things went badly wrong. A major portion of the fine old building simply gave way and collapsed, leaving this scene of devastation for all to see. The mighty beams that once helped hold its head high had given way and it came tumbling down to the ground in a cloud of dust. The Six Chimneys, named obviously for the pots that can still be seen on its roof in the picture, had been around for nearly 400 years. Built in 1566, it was truly a Tudor building. It stood at the junction of Kirkgate and Legh Street, the latter being a small alley that led to Peterson Road. In later life the ground floor was used for shops, including one that sold Hercules cycles during the interwar years. The whole area was redeveloped at the end of the 1960s and a roundabout put in place on this site.

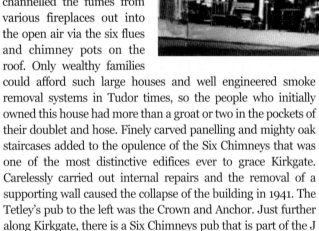

Below: The first pedestrian crossings with flashing yellow orbs were installed in the late 1930s during Leslie Hore-Belisha's time as Minister of Transport. The beacons have been named after him ever since. The markings on the road were simple studs, showing the path across the street for anyone wishing to cross. These crossings were one of the many road safety measures that were introduced in the 1930s as the government got to grips with the nation's poor record in this area. After World War II, it was acknowledged that car drivers were quite properly focussing their attention on the road and, although a bright yellow beacon on the pavement was distinctive, the presence of a crossing could be further recognised by street markings. In 1949, about 1,000 sites were earmarked for experimental use. Alternate blue and yellow strips were painted and a comparative study of accident statistics begun. This was so successful that, by 1951, all such pedestrian crossings had to have the two tone effect. The choice of black and white gave rise to the nickname of 'zebra crossing'. Dating from early in the 1950s, workmen are here preparing the installation of a zebra crossing at the Wood Street end of the Bull Ring. Various other creatures have given their names to crossings, for example the pelican, panda, tiger and toucan, but the zebra was there first.

Below: Wakefield's parish church became the Cathedral in 1888. The tower and 247 feet high spire together make it the tallest in the county. The former was recased in stone and the latter rebuilt in the late 1850s. Other restoration work around this time was overseen by George Gilbert Scott (1811-78). He was one of several generations of architects whose work was significant in shaping the face of many churches and municipal buildings in our towns and cities. The original building's size reflected both the prosperity and the degree of piety to be observed in the medieval town. Even as far back as the 12th century, the church that stood here was a large one for the times. Substantially rebuilt in the 14th century, the new stone church was consecrated in 1329. Its elevation to cathedral status took place at the same time as Wakefield became a city and a new diocese was formed. In the last century, some extension work has taken place, with that at the east end being a memorial to W W How, the first Bishop of Wakefield. Treacy Hall was built and named in honour of the eighth - Bishop Eric Treacy- some time after this photograph from the 1950s was taken.

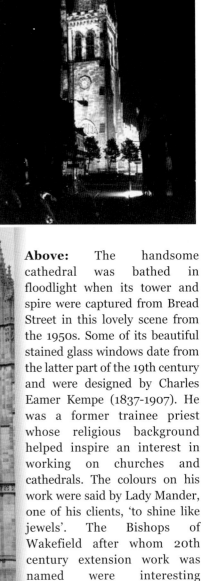

Above: The handsome cathedral was bathed in floodlight when its tower and spire were captured from Bread Street in this lovely scene from the 1950s. Some of its beautiful stained glass windows date from the latter part of the 19th century and were designed by Charles Eamer Kempe (1837-1907). He was a former trainee priest whose religious background helped inspire an interest in working on churches and cathedrals. The colours on his work were said by Lady Mander, one of his clients, 'to shine like jewels'. The Bishops of Wakefield after whom 20th century extension work was named were interesting characters. William Walsham How (1823-97), the very first incumbent, was happy with humble parish work for 30 years before gaining a modest promotion to the post of Bishop of Bedford, a job he held for nine years before arriving in

Wakefield in 1888. He wrote several books and hymns, but is better remembered in literary circles for joining in the condemnation of Thomas Hardy's 1895 novel, 'Jude the Obscure'. Referred to by some as 'Jude the Obscene', How was sufficiently angered by its content to be one of those who publicly burned copies of the book. Another Bishop, Eric Treacy (1907-78), was also known outside the church. He was an avid railway photographer. He held holy office in Keighley, Halifax and Pontefract before serving as Bishop of Wakefield from 1968 to 1976, but is best remembered for his collection of 12,000 images kept at the National Railway Museum. He must be the only bishop to have a locomotive, a former LMS black five number 45428, named after him. He died after a heart attack on Appleby Station platform.

Right: A 1910 view looking along Bread Street, which is situated off Marygate and is a direct route through to Northgate and the imposing Wakefield Cathedral. This was where the bread booths and bakehouse were located in the 18th and 19th centuries. It was originally called Rattan Street. Perhaps that is an indicator that cane products were woven along here at one time. However, the word might be a corruption of 'rotten', thus lending it whole new context. The old Cross Keys Inn stood to the right. The more elderly readers of this book may remember Bread Street as the HQ of Wakefield's Radio Relay. During the war years, the Radio Relay announcer would break into the BBC programmes to transmit the local air raid warning message.

The group pictured look somewhat surprised and transfixed by the camera. Maybe it was the first time they had seen anyone using a hand-held camera. In the early 1900's the Kodak Brownie camera was the first hand-held model that was

cheap enough and simple enough for even children to use, making photography accessible to the masses. Bread Street was closed in the spring of 1982 while renovation work was carried out with the intention of turning it into something atmospheric and nostalgic, along the lines of The Shambles in York, as an attempt to encourage tourism. A street party was held in June 1983 when it reopened.

The sun shone brightly on Teall Street shoppers and those making their way into the old market that dominates the left hand side of the road on a very pleasant summer's day. The new Market Hall that replaced it opened on 23 April, 1964. Here we can make out the Melbourne Ales public house and the Willow Pattern restaurant on the right. In the foreground is the kiosk that was occupied by G Whitehead, the tripe dresser. Now, this is not a reference to Mr Whitehead's appalling choice in clothes, but one made towards his trade. Tripe is one of those foodstuffs that you love or loathe. Some of us just adore Marmite, while the rest gag at the thought of it. The same is true of this edible offal. Usually, it is acquired from the chambers of a cow's stomach. Blanket or smooth tripe comes from the rumen, while the honeycomb variety is obtained from the reticulum. That it is popular in France when eaten as andouillette, a form of sausage, should be enough to put anyone off. Despite that, some readers will recommend the stuff or have seen their dads roll in from the local just after closing time and tuck in to a plateful of tripe and boiled onions. The former is liberally dosed with vinegar and the latter with butter. We do not think the dish appears in any of Delia's books.

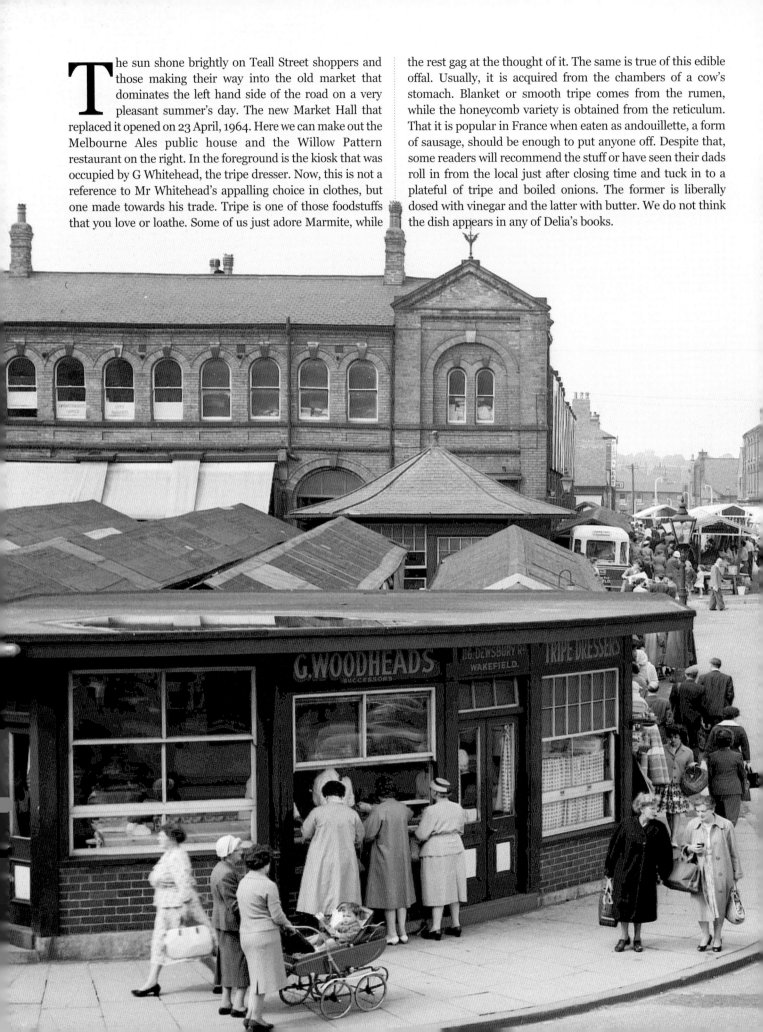

Above: Wood Street, as it looked in 1939, had John Crockatt, dyers and cleaners, on the left. The Mechanics Institute or Wakefield Museum is in the background, along with the Town Hall clock tower, Court House and County Hall that are all easily recognisable in this part of the city. The smart cars parked along one side of the road, with their distinctive mudguards, reliance on chrome for ornamentation and, in some cases, period running boards and side mounted spare wheels, would be mothballed before too long. When war was declared, only essential motoring was allowed and petrol rationing bit hard. Everyone understood the need to conserve fuel that was needed by our armed forces and by hauliers of our food supplies. Even so, the middle classes had become used to their toys and were a bit miffed that they had to walk or take public transport like the rest of us. We had more sympathy with their moans after peace was declared because petrol did not come off ration until 26 May 1950.

Right: This picture possibly taken just before the last war, is of the Express Newspaper Series offices on the corner of Southgate. The Wakefield Express was first published in 1852 and is the flagship title of the Yorkshire Weekly Newspaper Group, a division of Johnston Press since 1985. The Express centenary was commemorated in a documentary film made by Lindsay Anderson, the man who was a prime mover of the Free Cinema movement. Anderson was also the director of the 1963 movie, 'This Sporting Life'. When he made his 30 minute film about the Express, he was in transition between his work on industrial projects and his move into 'new wave' movies. He looked at the newspaper as being a reflection of that which was important to local society and that which represented the attitudes and values held by the city's inhabitants. His camera followed reporters as they travelled around the area in search of newsworthy events: a tea for the benefit of a local rugby team, a school concert, a constituency political meeting, the launching of a ship and the unveiling of a war memorial. Such happenings were of interest to residents in the area. If they wanted news from further afield, they bought a national newspaper or listened to the news on the Home Service.

Right: Even though this has all the appearance of a very modern photograph, it is in fact over 30 years old. Taken in 1975, at the junction of Northgate and Little Westgate, it shows quite clearly how the shopping environment had changed from the way we went about our tasks in the middle of the last century and in the years before that. The old, character laden buildings have gone. Removed like some diseased limb in a necessary amputation, many of the shops, stores, pubs and old houses were ripped out and discarded. The parallel only has limited acceptability. While it is true that some premises were worn out and had to be taken down, there were many others that required just a bit of careful tending. There was no need to cut down everything in sight. Had those responsible for the wanton destruction thought a little harder, could there not have been a harmonious marrying of styles? Instead, what did we get? If it had Edwardian, Victorian or Georgian in its pedigree, then bye-bye. In their wake came rectangular conformity that is boring to look at and depressing to work within. Pick up this style of city centre shops, malls, car parks and arcades and drop them into the centre of Slough and vice versa. Now, who would notice the difference?

Below: There were several fires in the 1960s and early 1970s at Rawson's Castle Bank Mills on Portobello Road. The textile industry is well used to the dangers of working with flammable materials and, to some degree, accepts that accidents will happen from time to time. This fire, like so many others, attracted a crowd of onlookers. Quite what they hoped to see is a mystery, but there must be something that we and moths both have in common in terms of flames and attraction. W E Rawson's company based on the banks of the River Calder and trading more recently as Rawson's Carpets, making fibre bonded products, used to process reconstituted wool made from rags which were reused in other textiles. It was founded in the late 19th century and is still a privately owned family business.

AT LEISURE

Below: This impressive Westgate building, seen in part of its glory years in the 1920s, was the city's former Corn Exchange. It was built in 1837 as a dealing house, but its first floor assembly rooms were in frequent demand in Victorian times for concerts, public meetings and bazaars. The ground floor of the Exchange was used as a roller skating rink in the early 1900s and, in 1910, the first floor was converted into the Grand Electric Cinema. Cinema goers were being invited to come and view 'The City of Pleasure', based on a 1907 novel by Arnold Bennett. He was a very popular figure, particularly well known for his work about 'the five towns' in the Potteries. The Grand Electric had its best days during the silent movie era and the years leading up to and just after the last war. As with many other cinemas, it fell victim to the twin assaults of bingo and television. Entertainment requirements changed as people found new ways in which to relax and enjoy themselves. In later times, Martin's Bank on the right became Betty's Snack Bar, but everything came to an end in 1963 when the buildings were demolished, taking away a historic part of Westgate. The Argos store now stands on this site.

Right: The Empire Theatre opened on Kirkgate in 1909 as a music hall, though this form of entertainment was waning in popularity. It began showing silent films during the Great War and by 1921 Rudolph Valentino, Mary Pickford and company were all the rage and the music hall acts became just a memory. It was converted into the Gaumont Cinema in 1931 just as talkies began to replace silent movies all over the world. This was the start of the golden age of cinema when every town had a host of picture palaces that were full to bursting all week and even turned patrons away at the weekend. Gaumont Cinemas established a British Junior Club for Boys and Girls in 1945, attracting hordes of youngsters to come along to Saturday morning shows. These were well attended right through to the start of the 1960s. Children enjoyed cowboy films with stories of Kit Carson, cliffhanger thrills and spills in serials featuring Buster Crabbe as Flash Gordon and the comedy of the Three Stooges, along with cartoons of Sylvester chasing Tweety Pie or Mr Magoo bumping into things. Wakefield used to

boast over a dozen such establishments in and around the city. Joe Haigh was the chief projectionist when 'Up Front' was the main feature film in 1951. Starring David Wayne and Tom Ewell, it was based on a wartime cartoon strip about two American soldiers on the Italian front. Ewell went on to star with Marilyn Monroe in 'The Seven Year Itch'. You got two films for the price of one back then. The second feature at the Gaumont was 'Cattle Drive', with Joel McCrea, Dean Stockwell and the remarkably named Chill Wills. The cinema was demolished in 1960.

Right: Young Jessie White was born in the 'noughties'. Seen in 1909, she was playing with her pram and dolls, just like any other five year old before or since. Sugar and spice and all things nice, Jessie would later marry Ernest Harrison. The two families were boot repairers in Westgate. The photograph was taken at the rear of the White's house and shop at 150-152 Westgate. Jessie was the daughter of James and Agnes White. Her mother was well known in the district for breeding Pomeranian dogs. Shoe and boot repair was a thriving business. In our modern throwaway society, we buy our footwear and discard it when it has come to the end of its days. Our parents and grandparents were much more prudent and would get far longer use out of their shoes and boots by having them resoled many times over.

us have all the fun we should have had when we were younger. Youth is wasted on the young. It should somehow be transferred to pensioners who just love to thumb their noses at petty bureaucracy. Of course, their children pull their hair out in despair as mum decides it is about time that she went for a parachute jump or when dad says that he has bought a Mazda MX-5 sports car. The grandchildren, though, just love the idea. Go for it, gramps. Of course, they are fed up with being told either to 'grow up' or to 'act your age'. How can you do both? Life is such a puzzle. This jolly generation gap was spotted in the 1950s at Priory House, Pontefract.

Above: There is an affinity between the very old and the very young. Little ones know no better and old 'uns could not give a toss. There is absolutely nothing wrong with being silly and 70. When you have had most of your life being told to conform to certain expected patterns of behaviour, it is great to be able to kick over the traces before you kick the bucket. By the time that your teeth and hair drop out you know that time is short, so let

Below: The horn of a gramophone sticking out of the top of the small pavilion is quite a Heath Robinson affair, but it probably served its purpose well enough. The spectators were enjoying the Sports Day at Normanton Grammar School. The males can be grouped according to their headgear. Largely working class types had the flat hats of their social standing, while more well to do chaps stood there under smart trilbies and homburgs. Boys of various sizes and ages wore their school caps with a mixture of pride and

embarrassment, dependent upon their ages. The school, situated on Church Lane, was founded in 1592 partly by money left in the will of John Freeston, of Altofts, and a further £1,000 donated by the late Thomas Ward. Local donations of £2,000 meant that the school could be sited on Mill Flat Field, the land having been purchased from the Vicar of Normanton. The school was rebuilt, and reopened on 1 November 1897 by the Earl of Crewe with Mr C W Atkinson as headmaster. He was succeeded by Mr L E Brittain and the campus was enlarged in 1905.

Above: Children lining up to watch a matinee at the Picture House on Westgate in 1943. The children could get in free if they brought old rags, tyres or paper to help in the war effort. Horse and carts are outside the cinema collecting the childrens donations.

Right: The Classic Cinema pictured in March 1977 was getting ready to reopen after being closed for some time. It was acquired by the Classic Cinema Group and reopened on Easter Day in 1977. Unfortunately it would close again the following year. However like many of the old picture houses it would open again some years later as a popular nightclub venue.

G one fishin', as Bing and Satchmo once duetted. This family group, pictured in 1961, had cycled to the lake at Walton Hall and it was very much the case of watching dad show how it was done. Quite why the children have not got their own rods is a mystery. Walton Hall is the former home of Charles Waterton, a 19th century explorer and naturalist. He converted the lake and surrounding parkland into what has been described as the world's first nature reserve. The Hall is now a hotel offering guests angling packages on the trout lake, as well as golf on the championship standard Waterton Park course. The first Walton Hall was built here in 1435 by Richard Waterton, though the ruins of the water gate are all that are left of the original building. During the Civil War, at the time of the siege of Sandal Castle, Walton Hall was subjected to some cannon fire from Parliamentarian forces, but survived without too much damage. In 1767, Thomas Waterton demolished the medieval hall, replacing it with the present one. His son Charles' collection of preserved birds and animals is kept in Wakefield Museum. Sadly, the next generation was headed by Edmund Waterton, a profligate individual who frittered away the family fortune to such an extent that he was declared bankrupt in 1876 and Walton Hall was put up for sale, having been in the family for over 400 years. Edward Simpson, a soap magnate, purchased the property in 1878. It was used as a military hospital during World War II, later being a maternity hospital before conversion to a hotel.

Above: Almshouse Lane is on the edge of the Ridings Shopping Centre and the name of the lane is an obvious reference to the almshouses built on it in 1646. The swimming baths where these ladies enjoyed a splash in the 1930s is no more. Between 1874 and 1938, this was the only public baths in the city until the one on Sun Lane opened. Baths were originally places for public cleansing, but with improvements in housing and domestic facilities that did away with tin baths in front of the fire and outside toilets in the back yard, swimming for pleasure became a popular pastime. This activity was given even greater publicity by the movie success gained by top class swimmers such as Johnny Weissmuller, Buster Crabbe and Esther Williams. Their watery exploits helped them to gain great fame and wealth thanks to their work on the silver screen. Weissmuller became Tarzan and Crabbe was Flash Gordon. Weissmuller won Olympic gold in 1924 and 1928 and Crabbe was a champion in 1932. Esther Williams won the American national title in the late 1930s and starred in a number of movies that had synchronised swimming sequences. These bathing belles at Almshouse Lane Baths might well have been inspired by the movie stars or perhaps they just enjoyed healthy exercise and the chance to get away from their husbands for a while. Nothing wrong with that.

Right: These kiddies in the playground on Ings Road in 1962 had grown up in the late 1950s as we came out of the postwar austerity phase that had many of us grumbling about just who had actually won the war. Although they would experience any number of governments and prime ministers, they would know just one monarch throughout the major portion of their complete lives. For them, white goods such as washing machines, fridge freezers and the like would be commonplace. They would never experience the difficulties of life in a house that was freezing cold in winter until dad had managed to struggle with sticks, newspaper and coal in the grate. They had hot water at the flick of a switch and shiny motorcars to whisk them off to the airport to enjoy their two weeks' package in the sun. Best of all, they would never experience cowering in a shelter as a Junkers or Heinkel droned overhead. Children in the second half of the 20th century enjoyed the sort of healthcare only available to those with a few bob in their pockets in earlier times. They know now that their elder siblings were baby boomers while they were the product of the' never had it so good' days. For them, most of their lives are wrapped up in what became a new Elizabethan age.

Left: The sideboard and wallpaper put this photograph into the period of the early 1950s. The lad with the guitar was perhaps taking his first steps to becoming a pop star. By the time he had reached his mid-30s he could have become part of Ossett's legendary pop group Black Lace, notable for their 1984 hit 'Agadoo' which got to number 2 in the UK charts. At the time this photo was taken Crooners such as Dickie Valentine and David Whitfield were performing to packed houses, but the guitar, washboard, drums and tea chest bass were about to become a force in the land. Skiffle was on its way. Nancy Whiskey would sing about her 'Freight Train', Johnny Duncan would warble about his 'Last Train to San Fernando' and, the daddy of them all, Lonnie Donegan, was about to let rip on the 'Rock Island Line'. Coincidentally, these three songs were all about the railways, but it was the style of song that made them stand out. The blend of blues, country and jazz, often played at a fairly frenetic tempo, was something to which youngsters could relate. Instrumentation was comparatively simple, so potential musicians found it easy to get to grips with the chords and melodies. Chas McDevitt, the Vipers and Wally Whyton were other exponents of skiffle who inspired others to pick up guitars and try their luck. In Liverpool, a group of teenagers formed a small combo called The Quarrymen. It was later to be renamed The Beatles.

ROYAL VISITS

Below: Queen Mary was famous for her remarkable headgear. Whatever it was she chose, then you could guarantee that it was distinctive. On this occasion, it was a huge, dramatic affair, with a posy of flowers at the front. All ladies wore hats when out and about, but few could match the royal style. On other days, she favoured toques. These variously coloured creations were just as eye catching, if not more so, as the most delightful of Ascot fashions. George V and Queen Mary made a grand tour of the industrial north during the summer of 1912. On 10 July they came to Wakefield, visiting several important employers and manufacturers. They took in George Craddock's Steel Wire and Rope Works, on Denby Dale Road, and Edward Sutcliffe's Belle Isle Maltings, among others. Here a large crowd assembled to see the royal couple when they visited Newmillerdam. This was a very special occasion for local inhabitants as it would be, in all probability, their only opportunity to see the monarch and his consort in the flesh. Note how close the onlookers were. There was little thought that given to the possibility that someone might wish to do harm to the visiting couple. It was a different world a century ago.

Below: Huge crowds flocked into the city centre to display loyalty to the King when he came to Wakefield two years prior to the Great War. George V took the throne on the death of his father, Edward VII, in 1910. As would be the case with his own second son, George was raised not expecting to become King one day. George joined the Royal Navy as a 12 year old and expected to make the sea his life. His elder brother, Albert Victor, was groomed for kingship even while their grandmother, Queen Victoria, still had many years of her reign still to fulfil. However, he fell ill during an influenza epidemic that swept the country and died in 1892, just a few weeks before he was due to marry Princess Mary of Teck. Queen Victoria approved of Mary as a future consort and put some pressure on George to marry her. The wedding took place in 1893 and, although something of an arranged marriage, the relationship was a happy one. The motorcade that brought George and Mary to Wakefield was an impressive affair. It was also a sign that the royal family could move with the times, for they now relied heavily on the internal combustion engine as a replacement for a coach and horses. The couple reigned for over a quarter of a century until George's death in 1936.

Above: Queen Mary was something of a character. Despite her Germanic roots, she was born and brought up in this country and became a popular figure with the British public. This was cemented when she and her husband changed their family name in 1917 from Saxe Coburg Gotha to Windsor, thus making a clean break with the foe we were then fighting. This was at the height of World War I and was seen as a positive move. It is hard to imagine the delight on the faces of the owners and staff at Farr and Son's antiques shop when they knew that they were about to receive the most important visitor ever to have crossed their threshold. They never stopped talking about the day that Queen Mary came to call. The shop was situated in Pontefract Castle's main guard on Castle Chain. The castle has a long and chequered past, including serious involvement in the Wars of the Roses as a Lancastrian stronghold. Richard III, while Duke of Gloucester, used Pontefract as one of his official residences. In 1483, during his brief two year reign, he had three of his political opponents executed in the castle. It was a royalist stronghold during the 17th century Civil War, but was demolished on command of Parliament. After some excavation work, Pontefract Corporation opened the castle as a public park in 1882.

Bottom: King George VI and Queen Elizabeth came to the city on 21 October 1937. This was Trafalgar Day, though not officially celebrated as such. Some 132 years earlier one of our finest national heroes, Horatio Nelson, lost his life just as he was about to savour his most famous victory in the series of battles waged against the enemy during the Napoleonic Wars. The royal couple were still in the early days of a reign that had been forced upon them by the abdication of Edward VIII in late 1936. A firm reactionary, Elizabeth was horrified by her brother-in-law's actions. For him to abandon his duties was bad enough, but it meant that her husband was pressed into service to assume a throne for which he was unprepared. The new king was a shy and diffident man who was afflicted with a stutter that worsened under stress. Like no consort before or since, Queen Elizabeth took the lead when out in public. Even here, she is the one taking the lead, doing the greeting and indulging in small talk. During the war she became the darling of the nation with her steadfast determination to stay within these shores when others would have run off to safety in some haven, such as Canada. It was the King who trailed in her wake, rather than vice versa.

Top right, facing page: Members of the family firm, Bagley Brothers, posed with the King and Queen who had honoured the company with a visit during their tour of the area in the autumn of 1937. The glassworks was situated by the canal at Knottingley. It was once the country's most successful glass manufacturer with a reputation for fine quality that stretched well beyond our shores. Cousins William and John Bagley established the company in 1871 to make glass bottles. William Bagley was well versed in this field having first hand experience since 1850 when, at the age of eight, he began work at Pilkington Brothers of St Helens. Childhood was a short and precious commodity in the 19th century. In 1912 the company branched out into the production of crystal and pressed glass in addition to

its traditional wares. In 1924, Bagley's exhibited at Wembley where Queen Mary bought some items from a range that was quickly renamed 'Queen's Choice'. In the 1930s, under the management of Stanley and Percy Bagley, a range of decorative glass bearing the trademark name of 'Crystaltynt' was introduced. This was to be a real moneyspinner. To mark the occasion of King George VI and Queen Elizabeth's visit, employees were presented with a special glass plate and souvenir booklet. Bagley's was taken over in 1975 by Jackson Glass and later still by Rockware Glass.

Below: Victoria Alexandra Alice Mary Windsor (1897-1965) was the third child and only daughter of George V and Queen Mary. Known to everyone as Princess Mary, she also later became the Countess of Harewood, following her marriage in 1922 to Henry, Viscount Lascelles. She was very close to her brother David, or Edward VIII as he became. Consequently, she declined to attend the wedding of her niece Elizabeth to Prince Philip in

Below: The Duke of Edinburgh paid a visit to Horbury, to the southwest of the city, in the early 1950s. It was one of the occasions when he was able to be himself, rather than just the consort of the monarch, falling in a few steps behind. Such a role in life could not have come easily to a redblooded male who had known command during active service in the Second World War. Born in 1921, he was a minor royal in the House of Schleswig Holstein Sonderburg Glucksburg. It is just as well that he did not become a professional soccer player. Imagine having that lot on the back of your shirt. As it was, he renounced his titles and adopted the surname of his maternal grandparents, thus becoming Philip Mountbatten shortly before his marriage to the future Queen Elizabeth II. He had the title of Duke of Edinburgh conferred on him just before their wedding day in 1947. Although he has a reputation for making unguarded comments, he is well regarded by the general public because of them rather than in spite of them. We like someone who speaks his mind and hang the consequences. However, there has never been one whiff of scandal relating to the 60-plus years that he has been wed.

1947 as she thought that her brother had been poorly treated by his successor's family during the abdication crisis. Mary inherited the title Princess Royal from her aunt, Louise, a year after the latter's death in 1931. She showed a keen interest in the British Red Cross and spent time during the Second World War visiting hospitals and rehabilitation centres. In 1945, she donned the uniform of the Women's Voluntary Service when paying a call at Pinderfields Hospital, on Aberford Road. During World War One, public buildings such as the Girls' High School, Heath Hall and Walton Hall became military hospitals. Pinderfields was similarly pressed into action during World War Two with added Nissen huts used as wards. After the death of her husband in 1947, Princess Mary continued to live at Harewood House and became Chancellor of Leeds University in 1951.

Above: There were some suggestions that the celebrations for Queen Elizabeth II's Silver Jubilee were going to be rather muted. There had been rumblings in the press and from some Labour politicians, notably Willie Hamilton, about the cost of the monarchy. This left wing Fife MP was a serial royal baiter and member of the awkward squad, but his comments and those of other anti monarchists seemed to galvanise the general public. During jubilee year, the Queen toured the county and received what can only be described as a right, royal welcome wherever she went. It was not until Wednesday, 13 July 1977 that she made it to Wakefield, over a month after the week set aside for national celebrations of her landmark as our sovereign. The timing did not diminish the joy showed by the crowds who piled in behind the crash barriers, keen to get a glimpse of the royal personage. Willie Hamilton was seen for the humbug he was when the jubilee parties matched those of the Coronation.

Right: On 10 June 1980, Princess Alexandra paid a most welcome visit to Normanton's Sleepeezee factory. The company claimed to be the first pocketed bed manufacturer to be awarded a Royal Warrant for supplying Her Majesty the Queen. The Princess is the daughter of the Duke of Kent, a younger brother of Edward VIII and George VI. Alexandra, born on Christmas Day 1936, was just five years of age when her father was killed in a plane crash. Her mother, Princess Marina, was the last foreign princess to marry into the British royal family. Alexandra was a bridesmaid at the wedding of Prince Philip to her cousin, the future Elizabeth II. She represented the monarch on several overseas tours, notably one to Australia in 1959. She served as the Chancellor of Lancaster University for over 40 years. In 1963, she married Angus Ogilvy in a ceremony that was televised from Westminster Abbey. Princess Alexandra is seldom in the spotlight these days and contents herself with supporting the English National Opera and several charities.

Above: Princess Alexandra was once sixth in the line of succession to the British throne, but as the years have rolled by she has slipped to thirty-third on the list. The crowds gathered to see her in 1980 were not too worried about pecking orders. They waited excitedly for a member of the royal family to arrive at County Hall because, after all, a royal was a royal. There was something still a little magical and special about those with supposed blue blood in their veins. Cynicism had been shown to be very much a minority view just three years earlier when the country celebrated the Queen's Silver Jubilee. This cheery collection of mums and kiddies were hell bent on giving their guest a rousing reception. Although they were supporters of the monarchy, they were not the deferential sort of earlier times and were just as likely to say 'Hiya' to the Princess as their forebears were to bow and scrape. The women on the right make an interesting fashion contrast with one in jeans and casual top, while the other sports a leopard print coat over a tailored dress.

Below: This was a familiar scene on streets up and down the country on the 29 July, 1981, celebrating the wedding of Prince Charles and Lady Diana Spencer. The couple were married at St Paul's Cathedral before an invited congregation of 3,500 and an estimated global TV audience of 750 million - making it the most popular programme ever broadcast. Britons enjoyed a national holiday decorating the streets with buntings and balloons, donning hats and waving Charles and Diana flags.

THE WAR YEARS

Below: We were not stupid people. Many were fooled for a short while when Neville Chamberlain came back from Munich in the autumn of 1938, clutching a little bit of paper that he said promised 'peace for our time'. Those who believed him were clutching at straws for all the prime minister had done was to abandon Czechoslovakia to its fate and give Hitler some breathing space to make further plans for expansion. Despite the German assurances, many people in the various civil defence units listened to Winston Churchill's warnings about the duplicity of the little dictator with the toothbrush moustache. Newsreel footage of the Spanish Civil War showed just how vicious a major conflict would be in its impact on the lives of citizens in their homes. The damage wreaked by fire after a bombing raid was a major fear for all. The Air Raid Precautions (ARP) divisions in Wakefield put on a demonstration on the banks of the Calder in October 1938 to demonstrate the power of the equipment available to them. Their powerful hoses sprayed 1,500 gallons of water per minute across the river in a public demonstration that tool place at Thornes Wharf, near the large mills that would be vulnerable if a fire storm resulted from a German air raid. Thankfully, the Wakefield ARP was not needed in this capacity during the war, but it worked flat out in other areas.

provision of such centres was made compulsory. A list of compulsory equipment was drawn up under the Coal Mines Act that included 'two or more small birds or mice for testing for carbon monoxide'. The Ings Road station was demolished in the late 1980s and the site is now marked by a blue plaque.

Below: Charlie Whitaker, the Mayor of Wakefield, inspected a parade of Auxiliary Territorial Service (ATS) personnel near County Hall on Wood Street during his 1941-42 term of office. The ATS played a most important role during World War II. It had its roots in the Women's Auxiliary Army Corps, founded in 1917, but was created in its own right on 9 September 1938, nearly a year before war was declared. The government decided that the ATS would be attached to the Territorial Army and the women serving would receive two thirds the pay of male soldiers. At first, they were given menial roles as cooks, clerks and storekeepers. When the balloon went up, as the outbreak of war was oddly described in some quarters, men left for Europe and the ATS members became much more important cogs in the wheel of war. They acted as backup for the RAF pilots on bombing missions as they tracked movement to and from targets, operated radar equipment, flew Spitfires from factories to airfields, drove munitions and supply wagons and handled ambulances in the dodgiest of situations as the Luftwaffe flew overhead. When all unmarried women in their 20s were conscripted in 1941, it became apparent to everyone, that the ATS was a force for Hitler to reckon with. More then 190,000 were enrolled by VE Day. The ATS was succeeded in peacetime by the Women's Royal Army Corps.

Above: They might look like some form of Cybermen in an episode of 'Doctor Who', but these chaps were no scary, villainous monsters. In fact, they were just the opposite. Based at the Miners' Rescue Station on Ings Road, the group was fully kitted out with all the paraphernalia needed to effect a life saving mission deep underground. The men had breathing apparatus, helmets, lamps, ropes, first aid kits and even knee pads to protect their own limbs when crawling through confined spaces. These brave miners put the wellbeing of others before their own safety and were prepared to risk life and limb in helping colleagues trapped in dangerous conditions hundreds of feet below. During one of their visits to the city, King George VI and Queen Elizabeth inspected the line up and could not help but be impressed by the dedication of these men. In the early days, there was no lack of volunteers to go down the mines in efforts to save fellow workers caught up in a roof fall or explosion, but many rescuers lost their lives in disorganised and fruitless rescue attempts. Although some rescue stations were set up in the late 19th century, it was not until 1911 that the

Manor Road, but no fatalities or injuries were recorded. The town's own Home Guard practised manoeuvres on the recreation ground and drilled in readiness to help out should the enemy invade. The popular BBC TV sitcom 'Dad's Army' made audiences laugh in the 1970s and 1980s. Repeats in later years were no less successful. The country's living rooms rocked to viewers' merriment at the antics of a Home Guard unit run by a pompous bank manager. Its members included old soldiers, an undertaker, a butcher and a trainee bank clerk. That much

Above: These military vehicles were part of the Air Raid Precautions fleet. The wagons rumbled along the cobbled setts of Westgate in late 1939. This was in the early days of the Second World War when we really did not know what to expect. As hostilities became inevitable, the summer months were given over to making preparations for what was to come. Gas masks were issued, air raid drills were held and civil defence groups made plans for their reaction to any invasion. At the start of September, many tens of thousands of children were sent by train and bus from the cities into more rural areas as evacuees during the organised movement of youngsters known as Operation Pied Piper. Those charged with staying at home to help in the defence of our realm as members of emergency services, wardens, guards etc practised hard as they set about making arrangements to safeguard vital centres. The early autumn was a busy time as they set about their work and truckloads of people and equipment trundled along our streets. However, there was little in the way of direct action and this period was known as the phoney war. That soon changed with a vengeance when the bullets flew, bombers filled the skies and shipping was sunk as 1940 unfolded.

Above right: Ossett was thankful that it suffered just a single air raid during the last war. On the evening of 16 September 1940, a line of 10 incendiary bombs blew out windows and damaged property around Hope Street and

was accurate. They were just the sort of people that volunteered to join a force entrusted with guarding key installations and sworn to protect those left at home by service personnel fighting overseas. The rest of the television series did not do them justice. The Home Guard was not the bumbling outfit it was portrayed to be. Admittedly, when initially formed as the Local Defence Volunteers, some of its early efforts were ridiculous. One platoon patrolled with imitation rifles once used in a Drury Lane production. Elsewhere

catapults were recommended as launching pads for petrol bombs and broomsticks were converted into pikes when knives were attached. The force was renamed the Home Guard in July 1940 and 250,000 men were enrolled. Although still handicapped by a shortage of weapons and resources, they trained with vigour and initiative.

Centre: This rather strange advertisement appeared in the Wakefield Express on Saturday, 23 September 1939. Just under three weeks earlier, families sat in their front rooms on that fateful first Sunday in the month, gathered around their wireless sets to listen to a broadcast they would never forget. Germany had been issued with an ultimatum by the British government demanding that it undertake a withdrawal of its forces from Poland. Neville Chamberlain, the Prime Minister, reported that 'I have to tell you now that no such undertaking has been received.' Later, the King broadcast to the Commonwealth saying that we 'commit our cause to God.' Among the speakers of fine words were those who saw the chance to earn a quick profit. O S Wain, based opposite the Cathedral, obviously saw a niche in the market. While everyone else was concerned that their children and other relatives had taken precautions against mustard gas and the like, Wain was very happy to make sure that man's best friend was properly protected, at a price. Gas masks for dogs, indeed, but no doubt some gullible souls forked out for them.

Bottom: Members of Wakefield City Fire Brigade were involved in a recruitment drive for volunteers to join in the Air Raid Precautions (ARP) programme that desperately needed people to join up at the start of the last war. They need not have worried, because Britons came forward in droves to do their bit for king and country. The ARP was actually formed in 1924 after the World War I Zeppelin attacks and the increasing range flown by aeroplanes. The experience of the citizens of Guernica, the little Basque village that was blown off the map in 1937 by the Condor division of the Luftwaffe in the Spanish Civil War, had heightened everyone's awareness of modern warfare. Air raid wardens were quickly recruited, along with men to join the Auxiliary Fire Service, and women were encouraged to volunteer for the Women's Voluntary Service, Red Cross and similar civil defence groups. Each officer on the fire appliance donned a gas mask to alert everyone to the need to be vigilant and carry such a safety measure whenever out and about. At the start of the war there was a real fear of chemical or germ warfare. Children carried theirs to school in little cases and practised in their classrooms so that they could put them on quickly should the need arise.

Congleton. No doubt modern day civil liberties and human rights groups would have a fit that our 'guests' should be forced to undertake such a hazardous pursuit. The attitude was somewhat different in the early 1940s. 'You dropped them, so you dig 'em up', was the mantra. There does seem to be some unarguable logic behind that sentiment. Thousands of unexploded bombs once littered our towns and countryside and, even today, there are occasions when the occasional one turns up. Some farmer ploughing a field or a developer excavating a building site comes across one and the bomb disposal squad is called in.

Above: Various prisoner of war camps were established in the 1940s to house members of mainly German and Italian armed forces captured in combat. One such base was at Comberbach in Cheshire. The caption to this photograph states that it shows German prisoners of war on unexploded bomb removal duties in

Below: Wakefield's worst air raid took place on 14 March, 1941, at 10.50pm. Two large bombs fell on Thornes Road. This picture taken at the rear of number 76 clearly shows the devastation caused by the attack. All the houses between numbers 38 and 104 and 151 and 232 Thornes Road were damaged or destroyed.

Below: There may have been a war on and food was rationed and in short supply, but every effort was made to see that the children did not go without, particularly on special occasions. There were times in World War II when we struggled to find enough to eat, but we got through all right in the end. Some of the grub served up was not the most appetising and relied

heavily on the imagination and skill of the housewife, but we did not starve. There was little in the way of fancy stuff. Rationing saw to that, with its four ounces of bacon, a shilling's worth of meat, eight ounces of sugar, two ounces of butter and a single egg per person per week. There was a heavy reliance on vegetables and the government issued practical advice and suggested menus for dishes, including the infamous Woolton pie, a revolting concoction of swedes, turnips and carrots, topped with potato pastry and served with a watery brown liquid that was supposed to be like gravy. At the start of the war, Britain was accustomed to importing 70 per cent of its foodstuffs. That figure included half the nation's meat needs. Things were very different for the next six years. The workers and managers at the Rotol Airscrew factory, in Ossett, pushed the boat out for the employees' children at the 1944 New Year party and made sure that they enjoyed the occasion. Rotol was well known for its three blade airscrew that was fitted to Hurricane fighter planes, helping improve take off times and adding several mph to the top flying speeds. Rotol was a particularly influential company in the period 1937-60.

Right: During World War II all sorts of essential and non-essential foods were rationed, as well as clothing, furniture and petrol. Before the second world war started Britain imported about 55 million tons of food a year from other countries. After war was declared in September 1939, the British government

had to cut down on the amount of food it brought in from abroad and decided to introduce a system of rationing. People were encouraged to provide their own food at home. The 'Dig for Victory' campaign started in October 1939 and called for every man and woman to keep an allotment. Lawns and flower-beds were turned into vegetable gardens. Chickens, rabbits, goats and pigs were reared in town parks and gardens. Ration books were issued to make sure everybody got a fair share. This contained coupons that had to be handed to the shop keepers every time rationed goods were bought. Food was was the first to be rationed. On 8 January 1940, bacon, butter and sugar were rationed. It wasn't just food that was rationed during World War II. Clothing rationing began on June 1st, 1941, two years after food rationing started. There was a shortage of materials to make clothes. People were also urged to 'Make do and mend' so that clothing factories and workers could be used to make items, such as parachutes and uniforms, needed in the battle against Germany. Every item of clothing was given a value in coupons. Each person was given 66 coupons to last them a year. Later it was reduced to 48 coupons. Children were allocated an extra 10 clothing coupons above the standard ration to allow for growing out of clothes during a year. This did not prevent children having to wear 'hand me downs' from older brothers and sisters. In a make do and mend environment, trousers and skirts were patched and darned, Old jumpers were unpicked and

the wool used to make new garments.

Rationing continued even after the war ended. Fourteen years of food rationing in Britain ended at midnight on 4 July 1954, when restrictions on the sale and purchase of meat and bacon were lifted.

Above: Railway Cottages, in Wrangbrook, the little village midway between Pontefract and Doncaster, was the scene of these celebrations in May 1945 when the residents held a street party to celebrate VE Day at the end of World War II. Victory in Europe had taken nearly six years to achieve. All that the children preparing to tuck in could remember of their young lives was being touched by shortages, fear and sadness. They were growing up surrounded by ration coupons, bomb craters and missing relatives. But those troubles were put to one side as they prepared to party. Every street in the country was like this one, bedecked with flags and bunting flying above trestle tables that had been borrowed from schools and church halls. Mums had pooled their meagre rations or blown a week's worth of food coupons to put on the best spread the children had ever feasted upon. The buns might have been on the dry side as egg powder was not quite the same as the real thing, but they were buns after all. After the celebratory tea someone found an old wind-up gramophone and put on a record of the hokey-cokey and everyone danced themselves silly. While they cleared away, the mothers sang quietly about bluebirds and Dover, shedding a small tear for those who never made it back for this or any other party.

Below left and right: The residents of North Street and Castle Street in Fryston, the little former mining village in Castleford, were just like all the others across the country on Victory in Europe (VE) Day. However, there is one exception in that we can see several young men in the photographs. Normally, these celebrations were attended just by women, children and grandpas as the dads and brothers were still waiting to be demobbed or would never be coming home at all. However, in such a community as this, many men stayed at home to carry out essential work down the mines. The end of hostilities in Europe was announced on 7 May 1945. After nearly six years of trial and turmoil, we could almost relax, though there was still a job to finish in the Far East. All over the land trestle tables were pulled out onto the pavements. Coloured strips of cloth were hung from lampposts and flags fluttered across window sills. Schoolrooms and church halls lent their tables and benches. Dining room chairs appeared outside the front

door and the street parties began in earnest. Neighbours had become even more reliant on each other during the years of deprivation. With rationing biting hard, they helped out with the loan of a cup of sugar, a little bit of dried egg or an outgrown frock. Now they were getting together to give their children the time of their lives. Hoarded ration coupons were pooled. Sandwiches were filled, cakes baked in the oven and homemade orangeade appeared as if by magic. The best drawer in the sideboard was raided for tablecloths and excited kiddies sat down and tucked in.

EVENTS & OCCASIONS

Below: A large majority of the crowd had no experience of a royal coronation. After all, it had been over 64 years since the last one when Victoria received the honour. Her son was crowned Edward VII in Westminster Abbey on 9 August, 1902, some 20 months after her death. The coronation had originally been fixed to take place two months earlier, but the King fell ill with appendicitis. At that time, this was a serious and life threatening illness. Many died on the operating table, but Edward recovered well, though his doctors kept a careful watch on him throughout the long coronation service. The scenes of joy across Wakefield were echoed all across the land. It was early in a new century and we had a new monarch to take us forward. Yet, we knew that this era would not be a lengthy one. Because of his mother's longevity, Edward's accession took place when he was nearly 60, making him the oldest person ever to take the throne. The current heir, Prince Charles, will break that record one day. Whether or not his coronation will cause such numbers to turn out and process along Wood Street is a moot point. Hopefully, there will be similar flag waving and cheering, but we will just have to wait and see.

Left: The noble queen was unveiled by Mayor H S Childe in the Bull Ring in 1905 in front of a crowd of many thousands who packed the area. This memorial to Victoria commemorated the life and service of our longest reigning monarch. She died in 1901, having been on the throne for over 63 years, and was seen as a symbol of all that was great about our once extensive empire. Unfortunately, the poor old lady has been messed about and not left in peace. On 10 July 1950 she was removed and re-sited in Clarence Park and this was to be her home until 1985 when she came back here. With the extensive makeover to this part of Wakefield being deemed necessary in recent times, she was off on her travels again to reappear in Castrop Rauxel Square in the city centre's civic quarter. Perhaps she can rest peacefully at long last.

Below: In February 1946, there was quite a lot of interest shown in the enthroning of the Right Reverend Henry McGowan as the new Bishop of Wakefield. A crowd of bystanders lined the street as the formal procession that included mace bearers, local dignitaries and representatives of the law made its way from the Town Hall to the Cathedral. Bishop McGowan became the Vicar of St Mark's Church, Birmingham, in 1923, before moving to the Emmanuel Church, in Southport, in 1925, where he stayed for six years. He returned to the midlands when he took up post in Aston Juxta, later becoming the Archdeacon of Aston. His tenure as the fifth Bishop of Wakefield lasted three years when he was succeeded by the Right Reverend Roger Plumpton Wilson. His son, Bruce, was appointed in 1973 as headmaster of Haberdashers' Aske's, one of the country's most successful direct grant schools.

Left: If you want to get ahead get a hat. This large group of ladies, sitting down to a formal meal in the Town Hall, showed quite clearly that is was the done thing to be wearing suitable headwear when attending any form of function. True, there was a small handful of those who attempted to be nonconformist, but, by and large, a real lady knew how to appear in public 70 years ago. To be seen outside when bareheaded was just not on. Why, that was almost as bad as smoking in the street. We were told in no uncertain terms that only a certain class of woman behaved like that. Quaintly, it was not just the middle classes and above who clung to such beliefs. Many working class women made sure that their hair was literally kept under wraps, even if it was just a headscarf that did the job.

Below: The Wakefield Pageant was organised by the local Chamber of Trade as a means of advertising business and commerce in the area. But 1933 was a difficult time in which to promote any form of trade and expansion. The country was in the grips of the depression years, with several million out of work and companies going to the wall on a daily basis. Belts were tightened as families faced long periods when there was little food on the table and the future seemed bleak with little to cheer them on the far horizon. The celebration of our history with processions and tableaux, like this one that featured performers dressed in medieval religious costumes, were blatant attempts to raise public morale during such hard times. Most of the pageant action took place in Clarence Park and some 3,000 local inhabitants are said to have participated in a series of 11 episodes that depicted our historical heritage. Wakefield dubbed 1933 as its 'Year of progress', though this was rather a fanciful notion.

Above: Ossett is a town once dominated by the 19th century stone mills that flourished when woollen waste was processed and the production of machinery for the textile industry bolstered the local economy. Cussons soap was also a major employer. It is quite likely that the youngsters in this 1950s picture scrubbed up with Imperial Leather and maybe one of two used the Sweet Seventeen range of cosmetics to enhance their appearance. The Ossett Carnival Queen held centre stage as she posed for an official photo shoot. Her attendants and page boys stood rather stiffly in the background. Several of the girls harboured secret ambitions to be the ones to wear the crown in subsequent years, though the boys wished that the earth would open and swallow them up. It was hardly the sort of thing to be boasted about on the playground on Monday morning. Mum might have been delighted with a shiny face and clean hands, but wearing satin and having your hair perfectly in place did not do much for the 1950s equivalent of street cred. To make matters worse, the scene was going to be plastered all over the local paper. The young lady, however, was more than pleased with her fame. It was a memory that would stay with her forever.

Top right: In case you are not sure, the Mayor, Councillor Mrs E H Crowe, is the lady in the centre who is wearing a hat. The ones flanking her were not flunkeys from the Town Hall but competitors in a beauty contest held in 1946. Beauty contests were very popular and seen by everyone as harmless fun. They were an extension of the selection of a carnival queen or pageant princess. Every town had its own champion who helped promote its business and keep its name in the public eye. Beauty queens enjoyed their moments in the limelight and were delighted to be called upon to open shops, offices and shows. As interest grew, each year a handful was able to use the title as Miss Smalltown to help move on to bigger things in the world of modelling or even movies. Eric Morley, a publicity manager for Mecca, spotted an opportunity and organised the first Miss World contest in 1951. Originally called the Festival Bikini Contest, as this was the year of the Festival of Britain, the new name was coined by the press and was quickly adopted by Morley. Kiki Hakansson, a Swedish lovely, was the first winner. Miss World was first televised in 1959 and attracted large audiences until the politically

correct lobby damaged its acceptability as appropriate entertainment. In 1961, Britain had its first winner when Rosemary Frankland was crowned. Sadly, her fame was shortlived and she battled with depression in later years and died, reportedly of a drug overdose, in 2000, aged just 57.

Right: In Upton, when Josie Jackson walked down the aisle in March 1945, she was accompanied by a trio of pretty young bridesmaids. Hours of intricate and painstaking work had gone into creating these outfits. They show just how imaginative and creative people could be. The war still had several months to run and rationing continued to bite hard. There was little in the way of clothing coupons that meant that a vast amount of money or material could be made available. What fabric there was had to be earmarked for parachutes, uniforms, hospital sheets and dressings and anything else deemed to be vital to help the war effort. Mums, sisters and friends did not let such little things as shortages get in the way of their wedding preparations. They commandeered net

curtains that once decorated the windows of their houses and had been replaced by blackout drapes. With the skill of seamstresses well used to creating the remarkable out of the basic, they went to work and produced the results we see here. The centre dress is retained for all to see in Wakefield Museum.

Above: On 5 June, 1971, Harold Wilson went walkabout in the crowd that had gathered to see him and witness the official opening of the new road bridge over the Aire and Calder

Navigation at Stanley Ferry. The bridge is close to the impressive aqueduct that was the world's largest cast iron aqueduct when it opened in 1839. An additional wider one was added alongside in 1981. Wilson came here as the Leader of the Opposition to Ted Heath's Conservative government. The Labour chief had served as our prime minister from 1964 to the summer of 1970. Born James Harold Wilson in 1916 in Huddersfield, he was to become one of the senior figures in British politics in the last century. His star first rose in the postwar Attlee government, becoming President of the Board of Trade at the tender age of 31. He served patiently in the queue for leadership of the Labour Party after Hugh Gaitskell succeeded Attlee. Wilson took over the reins in 1963. After losing out to Heath, he made a comeback four years later, winning the 1974 general election, but he resigned as prime minister in 1976. He continued to serve as a Member of Parliament until 1983 when he was created Baron Wilson of Rievaulx. He died in 1995 and a memorial service was held in his honour in Westminster Abbey.

Below: The view across Wakefield Show, thought to be seen in 1984, shows the usual tents, stalls and marquees that we associate with such an event. Here you can stroll along the lines of vegetable and flower displays, admiring the clever arrangements of sweet peas or the grandest leek that has been lovingly nurtured. There are craft stands, fancy cakes and the names of a teddy bear to guess. The Horbury Victoria Prize Band is playing and there is wine tasting to enjoy. A fairground has

been put up and visitors can enjoy trying to ring a plastic duck bobbing around in a bowl as they listen to Freddie Cannon blasting out 'Palisades Park' as the dodgems spark into life. We have not heard that song in years and memories of our youth come flooding back. There is sticky candy floss on our fingers and lips and our nostrils quiver as the aroma of fried onions drifts over from the hot dog stand. As we dodge the guy ropes holding the canvas in place, we take our grandson's hand and think wistfully back to the days when grandma was a lass and we rode on the waltzers with her. For those of us in the latter stages of life it is not the tunnel of love any more, just a jar of home made chutney to be shared, bought from the RSPCA stall.

Above: The children dancing round the maypole in front of the Cathedral steps in the mid-1980s were re-enacting a traditional scene that was for centuries part of village life, particularly at springtime. In some places the pole is a very tall one, often striped and decorated with painted flowers, ancient symbols and coloured flags. A good example of this can be found in Barwick in Elmet, the village just six miles east of Leeds. The more common maypole is a smaller one and, as here, sees dancers holding ribbons attached to it, weaving in and out of one another in an intricate fashion. The ribbons are intertwined and the dancers retrace their steps to disentangle them. At least, that is the theory.

Left: Shoppers on Teall Street stop to take in the show put on by the Boars Head Morris Men from Bradford. The dancing was part of the Middle Ages Festival held on 28 May, 1977.

WAKEFIELD TRINITY

In 1873 a group of young men from the local Holy Trinity Church formed the Wakefield Trinity club. Early matches were played on Heath Common, Manor Field and Elm Street before the move to Belle Vue in 1879. They were one of the initial 22 clubs to form the Northern Union after the acrimonious split from the Rugby Football Union in 1895.

Trinity won the Northern Union Challenge Cup for the first time in 1909, beating Hull 17-0 at Headingley. The result was reversed in the corresponding final in 1914, with Hull winning the game 6-0. This proved to be a precursor to Trinity's pre-war endeavours, as they went on to lose four Yorkshire Cup Finals in the thirties. The side included club stalwart Jonty Parkin who signed for

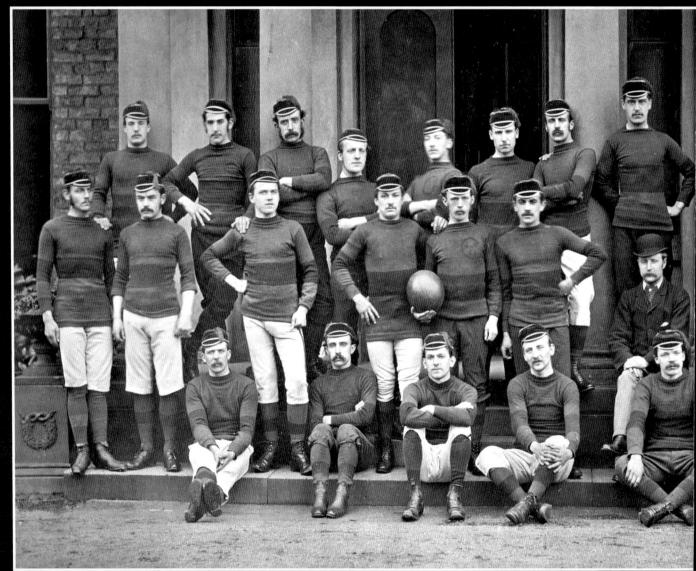

were adjusted shortly afterwards so a similar occurrence could not happen again.

Post War Years

The first Wembley final after the war produced a change of fortune for the Dreadnoughts and a return to winning ways, as they pipped Wigan 13-12 to lift the Cup. Earlier in the season, Trinity were the favourites to beat Bradford Northern in the Yorkshire Cup at Thrum Hall, but lost 5-2 in a very tight contest.

Trinity as a seventeen year old in 1913. Towards the end of his career Parkin made the headlines at the time by paying his own £100 transfer fee, so he could secure his release and join Hull KR. The game's by-laws

In the 1946 final, Billy Stott of Wakefield (pictured bottom row), was the first winner of the Lance Todd Trophy introduced in the memory of New Zealand born player Lance Todd, who died in a road accident during the second world war.

Trinity featured in the first league match to be broadcast on British television, a clash with Wigan at Central Park on January 12th, 1952.

The club was not destined to return to Wembley until 1960 and had to settle for the lesser prizes of two Yorkshire Cup and two Yorkshire League victories in the 1950's. When they did reach Wembley they scored an emphatic 38-5 win over Hull under the guidance of Ken Traill and loose forward Rocky Turner.

Above: *Pictured in 1947 are the Wakefield and Wigan sides with an impressive array of silverware. Both sides had achieved success in their respective counties as well as being Challenge Cup winners. Wakefield won the Challenge Cup in 1946, with a 13-12 win over Wigan, who won the trophy the following year.*

Top row: Baddeley, Higgins, Exley, Longley, Marson, Booth, Howes, Blan, Bratley, Atkinson, Blan, Shovaton, Ratcliff, Lawrenson, Banks, Ward, Woosey. Bottom row: Brooks, Banks, Perry, Stott, Wilkinson, Teall, Cunliffe, Mountford, Tooley and Nordgren.

Wakefield won their third post war Challenge Cup in 1962, running out 12-6 victors in a dour win over Huddersfield. The Fartowners went on to deny them the double a few days later in the Championship final at Odsal. During a purple patch Trinity also won the Yorkshire Cup final and the Yorkshire League.

Bottom left: Parading the Challenge Cup, 1960. **Above:** Going for the try line, action from the 1960 final. **Below:** Crowds gather in Wood Street for the civic reception given to the 1960 cup winners.

KR, but were again denied the double when Leeds beat them in the famous 1968 'water splash' final at Wembley. The match was played during a downpour and produced the most dramatic of finishes, when 'Man of the Match', Don Fox, missed a conversion with the last kick of the match which would have won the game for Trinity. Leeds were 11-10 winners.

Despite this lapse, Don was recognised as an outstanding kicker. Prior to joining Wakefield he propelled himself to third on Featherstone's all-time goal kicking ladder with 503 goals from

Wakefield achieved world wide fame in 1962, as many of the scenes from the film 'This Sporting Life' were filmed at Belle Vue Stadium, during Trinity's third round Challenge Cup match against Wigan. A gritty northern drama, the film tells the story of Frank Machin, a young and ambitious coal miner, who is on his way up as a rugby league star. Richard Harris who plays Machin, has said he considers it to be one of his finest roles. He certainly convincing, giving a powerful performance alongside Rachel Roberts, who is unforgettable as Machin's widowed landlady.

Despite winning the Challenge Cup for a fifth time in 1963, with a 25-10 victory over Wigan, Trinity were still unable to secure the league championship title. This milestone would finally be achieved in the 1966-67 season, when the experienced Harold Poynton led a powerful side to victory over St Helens in a replay.

In those days the North's professional rugby sides played in a giant single league of around 30 clubs. Not every team had the opportunity to play each other, so at the end of the season the top 16 clubs played in a series of of knockout matches culminating in the championship final.

They repeated the title feat again the following year against Hull

*Top left and top right: A poster and action shot from the highly acclaimed 1963 film 'This Sporting Life' starring Richard Harris. **Right:** Wakefield Trinity's victorious 1962 cup winning team.*

369 appearances, as well as a club record 162 tries. He was part of a legendary rugby league family and along with his brothers Neil and Peter, had strong ties to Wakefield Trinity.

Peter, after playing for Sharleston Rovers, had a 13-year playing career with Featherstone, Batley, Hull KR and Wakefield and became one of British rugby league's most successful coaches.

For his part, Neil Fox MBE (pictured left) became one of the most prominent figures in rugby league history, as he holds the the all-time points record, scoring 6,220 points from a total of 828 appearances in his career. As a goal kicking centre he scored a total of 4488 points for Wakefield. He is one of only two British rugby league players to have two testimonial matches. Both games were at Wakefield Trinity in 1966 and 1979. He was inducted into the Rugby League Hall of Fame in 1989.

It was over 10 years before Wakefield returned to Wembley under the guidance of Bill Kirkbride, losing narrowly 12-3 to Widnes in 1979, in front of almost 100,000 fans, with Wakefield's David Topliss winning the Lance Todd Trophy for Man of the Match.

The ensuing decline was temporarily halted when Wally Lewis signed up for a brief spell with the club. But even the presence of the mercurial Kangaroo couldn't prevent an inconsistent Wakefield from fluctuating between the two divisions. Former player David Topliss stabalised the Dreadnoughts' ship in the late eighties. He won immediate promotion in 1988 and consolidated the clubs top tier status by acquiring the services of seasoned internationals like Mark Graham, Steve Ella and Brian

Jackson as well as former Wakefield coach Andy Kelly.

David Topliss started his playing career at Normanton Juniors ARLFC before spending 13 years with Trinity from !968–81. He took over the No 6 jersey from another great player, Harold Poynton.

Wakefield were reduced to to lower division football with the arrival of Super league in 1995 but earned their place in the top flight on the back of a dramatic victory over Featherstone in the inaugural Division One Grand Final in 1998.

The team now known as the Wakefield Trinity Wildcats compete at the highest level in Super League each week...not bad considering their humble beginnings over 135 years ago.

Top: *Action from the famous 1968 'watersplash' final.*
Above: *Pictured in the mid 70's, from left to right: Former Wakefield player, Les Sheard, Mick Morgan, coach Peter Fox, and Trinity talisman, David 'toppo' Topliss.*

TRANSPORT

Below: The horse bus was the only real form of public transport for those wishing to get into the towns and city, unless they lived close to the railway. Alternatively, some horse buses were used as a link between a village and the nearest station. For these passengers in Newmillerdam in 1897, the transport world would change dramatically in just a few years. Before another decade was out, motorcars and trams would be common sights and the day of the horse consigned to the history books. The village is a quiet spot near Kettlethorpe Hall, the mansion built for the Pilkington family in the 18th century. Chevet Hall, a 16th century building restored by the Pilkingtons, was controversially demolished in the 1960s because it was said to be dangerous because of mining subsidence. Newmillerdam is best known for the country park created out of the former Pilkington estate. Wakefield Council bought the land in 1954, turning it into an amenity for the general public two years later. It is unlikely that anyone on this horse bus had ever set foot inside the Pilkington grounds. At one time, nine gamekeepers were employed with the specific purpose of keeping the intruders at bay.

Below: As is our custom, a knot of spectators collected to watch the workmen go about their job. Quite why we British like to stand and stare is a mystery, but we do, especially if someone else is doing the grafting. In 2009 men were digging up the Bull Ring as part of the regeneration plan for the city centre. This was part of the work carried out to revitalise this part of the city, along with Westmorland Street and The Springs, building on work already completed in the Crown Court Yard region. Wider pavements, greater greenery, a water feature and a reduction in traffic were all part of the scheme of things for the Bull Ring. Until 1847, it was here that a market was held and the prison and the Town Hall were sited. Over a century earlier, tramlines were being laid for the coming of electrification of the tram service. This replaced the horse bus service. Following its introduction in August 1904, it was immediately popular with people in suburbia who were able to get into and out of the city quickly, safely and in relative comfort. The trams stopped running in 1932 and the lines were dug up.

quite the 1920 equivalent of the stretch limousine as some charabancs were little more than lorries that were converted by having seats fitted to them. However, it was fun and that was all that mattered. These fine old days of motoring involved bowling along the open road, frightening cows in the fields as you passed by. The driver was a circumspect soul and acknowledged his responsibilities in transporting his passengers safely on their 'jolly'. A visit to the seaside was almost de rigueur. It might be to Scarborough that they were headed. There, visitors could enjoy the bright and breezy face of one of the country's most popular resorts and take a stroll along the front, make sandcastles on the beach or visit Peasholm Park. Those on the sands also enjoyed donkey rides, Punch and Judy and beach cricket matches. Later, they just sat back in deckchairs listening to the music from the bandstand before taking the ride back home to Ossett.

Above: Whether this was a works or pub outing is not clear, but we can be sure that they all had a good day out. Dressed in their best suits, frocks, warm coats and either caps or hats as befitted their social status, there would be some fine stories to be told if we are any judge of character. A ride on a motor coach, still a fairly recent phenomenon, became a rival to the day trip on the railway as it could provide door to door service. This was not

Bottom left: Dating from the 1910s era, the picture shows a tram has just stopped on the edge of Normanton Market Place. This small town to the northeast of Wakefield has quite a history. It was mentioned in the Domesday Book and, as can be seen by its name, had some significance for the Normans who gave Harold one in the eye at the battle of Hastings. The town was once surrounded by a moat and there is evidence that a motte and bailey fortification was built here in the 11th century. In more recent times, Normanton became well known as the focus of several lines in the early days of the railway. Normanton was unusual in that it was a small town linked with major cities across the country. For a while, it also boasted the world's longest station platform, at nearly a quarter of a mile in length. An abundance of clay and coal in the area helped Normanton flourish as a centre for brick making and its importance in the industrial north of England belied its size in terms of population. Queen Victoria stayed at the Station Hotel during a visit to the area and Dom Pedro, the Emperor of Brazil, paid a visit in 1871. Market Place was a good place to meet friends and have a gossip as it was the focal point of the town.

Above: Westgate Railway Station opened in 1867. The buildings seen here were demolished a century later and a living part of local history went as well. Although it opened after Kirkgate, Westgate has become Wakefield's principal station. Kirkgate was opened in 1840 by the Manchester and Leeds Railway Company, but now looks in need of some TLC. Westgate, on the other hand, is at the centre of modernisation plans. Occasionally, actor David Jason can be seen on the platform as Westgate doubles as Denton Station in the TV series 'A Touch of Frost'. When photographed, the clock tower and canopy provided a handsome sight. The railway was a marvellous invention and changed the lives of people the length and breadth of the nation. Families who had lived in one small district for several generations were suddenly able to pull up their roots and relocate as they sought work to better themselves. All of a sudden, a journey that once took several days by road could be covered in a matter of hours. People could visit relatives in other parts of the country, rather than having to take a holiday in order to do so.

Below: The 'Diamond Jubilee' locomotive pulls out of Wakefield Westgate station whilst hauling 'The White Rose' train.

Above: It is a lot easier to cross Westgate nowadays than it was over 60 years ago. On 8 January 1949, this woman took her life in her hands as she darted across the busy road. No fewer than five buses can be seen in this photograph, a sign of the times. Petrol for private motoring was still in short supply and rationing was in force until 1950. The black market did good business and spivs, with their little moustaches and slicked back hair, a bit like Private Walker in 'Dad's Army', had a field day. Cars were expensive for the ordinary man in the street to purchase and maintain. The family saloon would not be commonplace for the best part of another decade. Consequently, the bus was a favoured mode of travel. Most were handled by two person crews, featuring a driver and conductor. With the former marooned in his cab, the conductor was left alone to collect fares, issue tickets, ring the bell to alert the driver when to stop or go and deal with the inspector who might hop aboard unannounced to check that everything was in order. The bus on the left carried an advert for Vernon's football pools. This is one of the top companies in that line of gambling and is based near Aintree, Liverpool. Several employees formed themselves into a pop group, the Vernons Girls, that had some success in the late 1950s.

Right: Keighley and Worth Valley Railway is a five mile-long-track that runs from Keighley to Oxenhope and is perhaps the only current heritage branch line operating in its original form. On 12 August 1977, just as the gentry were off to enjoy the start of the grouse shooting season, this group of retired men from the Belle Vue railway works paid a visit to Keighley to renew acquaintance with a former Silkstone Colliery branch line locomotive that had been lovingly restored and put back to work. As if to offer a welcoming word, the locomotive let forth a gush of steam just as the photographer closed his shutter. Although modern trains are much cleaner and quicker than those of the past, there is something so reassuring and comforting about seeing and hearing the head of steam being raised. Even little children still go 'chuff chuff' when they play at being a train, despite being donkeys' years out of date. Those of us who can recall the days before Dr Beeching took his axe to our branch lines in the mid 1960s will remember glorious days when we left home after breakfast. Carrying our lunch in a school satchel, along with a bottle of Corona cream soda that had been brought by the delivery man the night before, we disappeared until tea time. We returned covered in specks of soot, but happy that a grubby notebook was filled with entries such as D1/3 D2957 (small shunter). Bletchley Park would have had trouble decoding that!

Right: This was one of the veteran cars taking part in what was billed as the 'Cavalcade of the Century'. To be picky, it should have been referred to as a motorcade as there was not a horse in sight, but we will let that pass; almost. The cars that lined up outside the Town Hall on 9 May 1960 represented motoring as it was in the early years of the last century. Nostalgia twinkled in every piece of polished chrome and the sheer joy on the faces of the motorists was a joy to behold. Never mind that the drivers and their passengers were wrapped up against the elements or had to endure something of a bumpy ride, this was true seat-of-your-pants motoring. Many put on period costumes to add that extra something as they set off along Wood Street. Some imagined that they were modern day Mr Toads, whizzing along country lanes. However, we sincerely hope that they did not

steal their jalopies, indulge in breaking speed limits and serve a jail sentence like the character from 'Wind in the Willows'. More likely, the behaviour was more akin to that observed in the 1953 movie 'Genevieve' about the London to Brighton veteran car run that featured a 1904 Darracq and a Spyker from the same year. You can almost hear Larry Adler's haunting harmonica theme to that film just by looking at this photograph.

THOSE WERE THE DAYS!

Each generation thinks of itself as modern at every stage of life and yet we are all relics and mementoes of our own history. As time goes by, we try to hang on to our more modish and fashionable behaviour and attitudes, sometimes with the thought that we can defy the passing of time with our constant recreation of 'the past'. Even so, most people enjoy looking back and remembering with affection things done or achieved and comparing the context of their early lives with improvements sometimes made in more recent times. Things often seem not to be as good as in the 'olden days', but most of the time we are not looking at a level playing field. Inevitably, many of our childhood memories, whatever our age now, are of endless summers and snow-filled winters, a sort of historically appropriate version of Dylan Thomas's 'A Child's Christmas in Wales'. But, for all of us, time marches on and, as we get older, it seems strange that we find ourselves attempting to explain to a nine year old god-daughter that there was life of a sort before computers, emphasising simultaneously our incredibly ancient origins! Wartime experiences and memories often define generations, although with involvement in more recent conflicts, even this timeline has had to be redefined. The progress in radio and TV development has outstripped most people's imagination and provided a sometimes obsessive and questionable way of filling our days. Until the middle of the 20th century, children often had to use their own imagination, inventiveness and creativity. The streets were filled with groups of children of different ages pretending to be somebody, somewhere and something else. This was fun for most, freeing and gentle in its stimulation, and engendered a relevant and satisfactory competitiveness conducive to learning.

This page: Outdoors including in the playground, improvisation was the name of the game. You didn't need a ball for football - a tightly bound bundle of rags or clothes would do. There were games that matched the seasons, conkers for example. Those determined to win used foul and dishonest ways to convert the simple conker into a hard and unyielding boulder to cheat their way to success. Later in the year it was marbles with those wonderful glass beads put to aggressive and

needy. The people in the picture are, from left to right, EE Bell, Harry Barnet, Mr Blakely and Charlie Shaw, with Bob Hodgkinson seated. The names of the children are unknown.

Below centre: In the 1950s, toys were still quite simple, for boys and girls. In a society that continued to place the emphasis on women as home makers and child producers, toymakers were still making a lot of money from selling pretty little dolls to pretty little girls, banking on their softness for small, defenceless creatures in their own image. This wonderful picture, taken in 1950, shows two such little girls enjoying posing for a 'family' photograph, repeated no doubt twenty years later as the real thing. Note the grittily determined, no-nonsense expression of the young lady at the back and the rather shyer, slightly myopic expression of the seated young lady with hair that, possibly, she has spent the rest of her life not being able to 'do a thing with'!

Below: The influence of Errol Flynn in the 1940s is obvious here in a game involving bows and arrows. His playing of Robin Hood against Olivia de Havilland as Maid Marian had a ground-breaking impact for some little boys that remained with them to their teenage years (and in some cases even longer!). Cinema has always had an influence on children's re-enactment and performance of stories and fables. Certainly children in the 1940s rarely complained about boredom or having nothing to do. They simply grasped the nettle and worked out what they could turn it into and did it together.

destructive use to determine who was top dog. There were also collecting activities, usually involving cards with familiar faces, often of footballers or film stars. Playground games were often determined by gender, with the differences usually marked by the polarising of physical prowess and single-mindedness on the one hand and a softer camaraderie and togetherness on the other. All the equipment and artefacts used in play were simple, often loud and often extremely irritating in their use and application, but great fun!

Above: Many Bethel Chapels follow the mission statement, 'to turn the lost into the found and the faithless into the faithful'. The word 'Bethel' is taken from two Hebrew words, 'bêt'and 'el', meaning the house of God. 'Chapel' is derived from the Latin 'cappella', meaning cloak. The building, therefore, provided a secret place where dissenters could worship God. Chapels were originally breakaway places, shattering the mould by providing a place of worship for those who objected to the status quo. In the dark days of the 1920s, poverty was rife. Many poor families had little in the way of either hope or sustenance. They simply got poorer. This soup kitchen at Bethel Chapel, New Brunswick Street, just off Thornes Lane, offered a form of gruel and bread to the

Right: The group of unknown kiddies, pictured here in the late 19th century, were the lucky ones. Dressed up in their finery, including the borrowing of a few fathers' flat caps, they looked the picture of health. In all probability, they would live to a ripe old age. Some of their siblings were not so fortunate. Insanitary living conditions for the working classes, poor diets and no such things as antibiotics, penicillin or mass immunisation meant that youngsters fell prey to a host of childhood diseases. Scarlet fever, whooping cough and measles, to name but a few.

was brought inside on a Saturday night, whether you needed an all over scrub or not. Waiting in front of a roaring fire, with kettles of boiling water being prepared, was part of the routine. This little lass obviously had her own individual model. Young Doreen or Dorothy, whatever her name was, could make the fun of bathtime last right up to the final 'Come on young lady, beddie-byes' was repeated in an exasperated voice.

Above: Little pedal cars were all the rage, especially for young boys, in the 1930s. Motoring was booming and toy manufacturers spotted the opportunity of a new niche in the market. While less affluent parents bought their children scooters for Christmas, Santa Claus packed his sleigh with imitations of real motorcars for the offspring of the wealthy. Some cars actually featured windows that really moved, working horns and lights, real chrome, bonnet ornaments, white wall tyres and custom paint. Many of the cars were made from metal, though this became less likely in the 1940s as the war effort demanded that such materials were channelled into the manufacture of military ordnance.

Right: Even in the middle of the last century, not all homes had bathrooms. Some of the older properties relied on outside toilets and the tin bath in the yard that

Below: Conditions may have been grim on occasions but there was usually time for a warm smile and friendly chat in the street. These were the days when people routinely left their doors unlocked or open, without fear of someone running off with their television. Of course, they didn't have a television, but you know what we mean! These days the neighbourly culture which we used to take for granted has disappeared from many areas and some people seem to know the characters in the popular soap operas better than the people next door. It would be unusual, to say the least, to see a modern housewife scrubbing the pavement outside her house in this day and age.

Top right and right: At one time, Monday was the traditional washday for many. For working class families, the burden fell upon mum. Her role as a housewife meant that the day was spent boiling clothes in a tub and wringing them out through the mangle before pegging out on the line in a back yard, or similar. Before the days of sophisticated washing powders and rubber gloves, reddened hands were her reward and yet there were still beds to be made, carpets to beat and lino to wash. The children needed feeding and the evening meal had to be ready when dad got home. It was hard work and there were few, if any, modern electrical

appliances or white goods to make the task of running the house any easier. Many families lived in terraced housing, some of it back to back, with outdoor lavvies, where you learned to whistle

with one foot against the door in case someone else attempted to enter this little smelly enclave of privacy. Many houses still had a tin bath that was dragged in from the yard and filled with kettle after kettle of boiling water before family members took it in turn to soak themselves. This photograph, dating from the 1950s, shows a typical scene from life at the time; families and communities were close knit, sharing each other's joys and sorrows. It was quite common to lend a neighbour a helping hand in times of need and this was often more than just a cup of sugar. Friendships were formed that lasted a lifetime.

This page: It was the Victorians who helped popularise the beach holiday when steam trains opened up the coastline for mill and factory workers to take their annual leave at Scarborough or Blackpool. Until then, such resorts were either out of reach or lay undeveloped. By the early 20th century, the seaside was a good place to indulge in a little naughtiness as young men showed off their muscles and young ladies displayed flesh that was normally hidden away under tightly laced corsets and voluminous skirts. The two cuties under the parasol look to be taking a particular coquettish delight in baring that which their mums never dared do outside the bedroom. Even then, the lights had to be off. The pair of young men often fancied themselves as the sort to get the girls' pulse racing. Let us face it, which red blooded female would not be driven wild with frenzy at the sight of those knees or the manly pose of the one with hands on hips, suggesting he was up for it, as they say today?

Fryston men were, and still are, all charm and machismo. The lady posing alone, though very fetching, failed to catch the attention of the deck chair attendant. A true northerner, he wanted cash first and voyeurism later.

Facing page, centre: On the beach, on those odd days that the sun shone, we largely made up our own entertainment. There were the traditional donkey rides and Punch and Judy shows that we paid to enjoy, but the rest of the time was spent in amusing ourselves. Apart from the obvious splashing about and swimming in the sea, every family had a cricket bat, tennis ball and set of stumps. Miniature Ashes Tests were played. Ornate sand castles were created and dad was the long suffering sort who did not mind too much being buried in the sand, yet again. Mini Olympics were organised with obstacle races, three legged events, leap frog games and stone skimming tourneys. Youngsters wandered off to explore rock pools and fill little buckets with crabs and other sea creatures. Adventurous kiddies disappeared for hours, but we knew that they would be safe.

Right: Who cared if the sun shone or the heavens opened? We had come to the seaside, paid our tanner for the deckchair and claimed our spot on the beach. Here we were going to stay for the rest of the day, hail, rain or shine. Our only acknowledgement that the weather would have any effect upon us was if we had to put on a raincoat or turn up a collar if the wind blew too hard. For the best part of the year, our fingers had been worked to the bone slaving over looms and shuttles or hewing coal from seams deep underground. When the annual holiday week, or fortnight if you were very lucky, came around, families packed their buckets and spades and made for the seaside, often finding their

Lancashire that they returned for their recreation each summer. Of course, anyone could go and paddle in the sea, but it had not always been so. There was a time when certain stretches of coast were reserved at particular times of the year. In 1900, a railway poster stated that sea bathing time at parts of Fleetwood and Blackpool had been set aside for the working classes on several weekends.

way to the same guest house that they had used the year before, and the year before that as well. Even if the landlady was a bit on the forbidding side, with her rules and regulations and 6.30 sharp message for the evening meal, it was the consistency that was liked.

Right: The family group posing in 1947 with Blackpool Tower as a backdrop had been here many times over the years. The place acted like a magnet for holidaymakers. The menfolk may have seen active service in the desert sands of North Africa, but it was to the beaches of

Above: When the baby boomer generation went to school in the early 1950s, it had benefited from the 1944 Education Act that brought free education to all primary and secondary aged children. For the first time, there was a level playing field, to use a school based analogy. Of course, that field had its bumps and muddy portions because perfection and complete equality could not be guaranteed. Those going to school in leafy suburbs tended to do better than those where slag heaps overlooked the grimy villages. But, at least working class kids had the chance of better and further education. Such lofty thoughts were not in the minds of youngsters enjoying the playground at Ossett's Spa Street County Primary School. The lad in the background obviously fancied himself as Roy Rogers or Tom Mix as he played on the rocking horse and checked behind him that pesky injuns were not on his trail. The girls, of course, enjoyed dressing the dolls as another couple had fun on the see-saw. They did not bump it too hard as the lads did when they had their turn.

Right: These lads, photographed in the mid 1950s, went to Queen Elizabeth Grammar School. From the look of them, it would seem that they were part of the Junior School. This fee paying establishment was just one of many that gave those families with money to spare a flying start when it came to their children's education. No-one spoke of equality under the 1944 Act here. It was a daily routine of cramming for the 11 plus as passing that was the be all and end all. Art, music, drama and science could wait. It was inky fingers, dip pens, sitting still and following rules. Education was not to be enjoyed but endured. The best days of your life? Pass.

Above: Out of necessity, road safety has become a major issue for all of us in our lifetimes and has been written into the school curriculum since the middle of the 20th century. As we can see in photographs from earlier in the last century that appear in this book, children played games in the streets and rode their bicycles on the carriageway with little danger to life or limb. With the steadily increasing traffic in the 1930s, safety became an obvious and challenging issue and, with accident statistics rising alarmingly, the government of the day was obliged to take action. Driving tests were introduced, Belisha Beacon crossings appeared in towns and cities and that well-known bestseller, The Highway Code, was formulated and published. In this photograph taken in 1950, youngsters are given instruction on a model roadway system. Stop, look and listen were watchwords drummed into children together with instruction on how to signal correctly and how to use crossings safely. In later years, we saw the Tufty Club, the Green Cross Code and, frighteningly, a fully permed Kevin Keegan advising us on why it was NOT a good idea to run out from behind parked cars! Sometimes, it all seemed a little light-hearted, but at least it got the point over.

Right: When Ernest Evans asked whether it was a bird or a plane up there and answered himself by telling us that it was a twister, a craze was born that swept dance floors across the western world. He also made sure that countless numbers of children would be embarrassed at weddings, 21st dos and parties during the 1990s as their parents risked hernias and heart attacks attempting to twist the night away whilst their offspring raised their eyes to heaven. Evans was a fan of the 1950s rocker Fats Domino and used his name as the inspiration for becoming known as Chubby Checker. Oddly, his first big hit in Britain was in 1963 with 'Let's Twist Again', a follow up to 'The Twist', a record that only became very popular the following year. By 1963, when this couple attempted to keep their seams straight as they gyrated in the front room to the music from their Dansette record player,

BIRD'S EYE VIEW

This 1961 photograph was taken from the roof of the Town Hall. A good head for heights was just as important as a fine camera in taking such a shot. Looking down Wood Street, the spire of the Cathedral pointed heavenward above the buildings below. In the distance, the cooling towers spewed clouds of steam and smoke out over the surrounding environment. The cars parked along the street show how tolerant of them we were in those days. Meters and the maids who tended them were a new phenomenon in Britain. Introduced in Oklahoma City in 1935, the dreaded contraptions only made their way to London in 1958. We all sympathised with Paul Newman in the movie 'Cool Hand Luke' when he went on a rampage and smashed up a streetful of the dratted things.

akefield Prison, a category A men's prison, was established as a house of correction in 1594, though most of the buildings in use today date from the 19th century. On a lighter note, the children's rhyme 'Here we go round the mulberry bush' is supposed to originate from the days when female inmates paraded around the mulberry tree in the prison yard. Some of the more notorious inmates who have been incarcerated here include Michael Sams, the murderer and kidnapper, Harold Shipman, the doctor who was a serial killer, Charles Bronson, described as 'the most violent man in Britain', and the spy, Karl Fuchs. Taken in 1952, the view includes the area between Darnley and Balne Lane, as well as the allotments where the library now stands.

As with many aerial views of the city, it is the Cathedral that stands out amongst all the other buildings that surround it. This scene, dating from 1963, is no different. Perhaps this is only proper, because it is here that people have come together to worship for the last 1,000 years. It has long been the focal point for pilgrims from far and wide. Even those without any real form of religious persuasion are drawn to this architectural gem and admire its beauty and impressive stature. The Cathedral Church of All Saints Wakefield, to give its true title, has every right to claim centre stage.

Bottom: The then new bus station and the remodelled Bull Ring, with its handsome roundabout, shouted out modernity in 1952. Britain was still in the grip of austerity, but some rebuilding and redevelopment work was undertaken. It was not before time as plans had been put on ice since the late 1930s when the nation's interests were necessarily refocused onto things more pressing. German jackboots marching into Poland made sure of that. The bus station, next to Marsh Way and the new market, was rebuilt in 2001 with a main passenger concourse and 24 bus stands.

Right: By 1964, there were a number of open sites dedicated to parking for private cars. Already, the growth in private motoring had become a major headache for Wakefield and all other towns and cities up and down the land. The erection of multi-storey parking facilities was seen as one solution to the increased demand on our roads, but this created as many problems as it solved. With this facility to accommodate more cars, the number of vehicles entering town increased, thus jamming the highways even more. The modern cost of car parking has become prohibitive. Naturally, this annoys city centre retailers who see trade being driven out of town.

Left: Looking across the railway line and into the city, the 1971 scene includes several high rise towers of flats. In the main, they had become the traditional council answer to providing low cost housing for those members of society who lacked the means or desire to own their own property. They were cheaper to build and maintain than an equivalent number of houses, but they came with a social price. Quite often, they were populated by a disproportionate number of families with anti-social attitudes. Christened 'slums in the sky', some became no go areas for the law abiding. In too many cases, they were hurriedly built and structural decay set in as quickly as its moral equivalent.

Below: To the left of Queen Street car park, the Mecca Locarno was one of the best night spots of the middle of the last century. As a dance hall, it had few equals in the area. Big bands performed quicksteps and excuse me waltzes were played, offering a lad the chance to cut in for a few moments with the prettiest girl in the room. With the coming of the pop groups in the early 1960s, fads changed. There was still live music from local artists and visiting performers, such as the Crestas, Susan Maughan, Shane Fenton and Helen Shapiro who came along, but before long the idea of a night out in a dance hall became passé. Even the sprung maple dance floor, lit with six clusters of three 1,000 watt floodlights, lost its sparkle. Using huge Strand Electric Sunset Dimmers, the lights switched between pink, magenta and red depending on the mood of the music, but they faded for the last time and were eventually lost under the Ridings Shopping Centre.

Above: The Market Hall and the stalls in the outdoor market were objects of intense activity in their heyday. During the hours of trading, there was a constant hustle and bustle, an ongoing drone of chatter that was punctuated by the cries of the traders promoting their wares. Each competed with a neighbour to get the housewives' attention. Either an eye catching gimmick or a quick line in banter was the best ways to attract customers. After that, it was a mixture of the quality of the goods and the sales patter used that would close the deal. For those who held the purse strings, it was part and parcel of the routine of shopping, but for the stallholder it was a way of life.

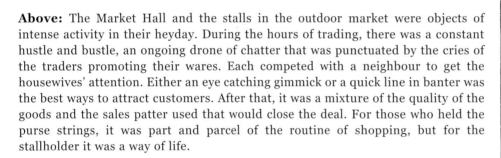

Right: Marsh Way opened in 1968 and, as well as providing Wakefield with a mixture of a feeder and ring road, it created something of a barrier between the city centre and its neighbourhoods. It did ease traffic movement into and around the area, but has now been targeted for remodelling under the regeneration scheme that got under way in 2007. Pictured in 1972, the city outskirts look to be remarkably quiet, with traffic that can only be described as flowing gently. Oh how we wish we could have said that on more occasions in the intervening 35 years or so.

AT WORK

Below: Charles Roberts and Company of Wakefield manufactured railway engines. It also had a major interest in Wagon Repairs Limited, a company that was founded in Rotherham in 1918. These engineers could both create and repair the locomotives, cornering a fair slice of the market for themselves. It did not matter, as there was plenty to go round. In those days the railways were a major industry and the great days of steam were far from over. In the 1950s, Sir Bernard Docker, the son of one of Wagon Repairs Limited's leading lights, found notoriety with his wife, Lady Norah, as free spending socialites. Their wealth was far removed from the modest wages earned by the men photographed in about 1912. Charles Roberts had his main works at Horbury Junction. Having contributed to the national economy as a major manufacturer of railway engines and rolling stock, the company turned its attention to the war effort in 1939 when it began to convert its plant for the production of Churchill tanks, or the Mark IV (A22) as they were officially known. The first ones came off the production lines in 1941. They were not an immediate success as they were

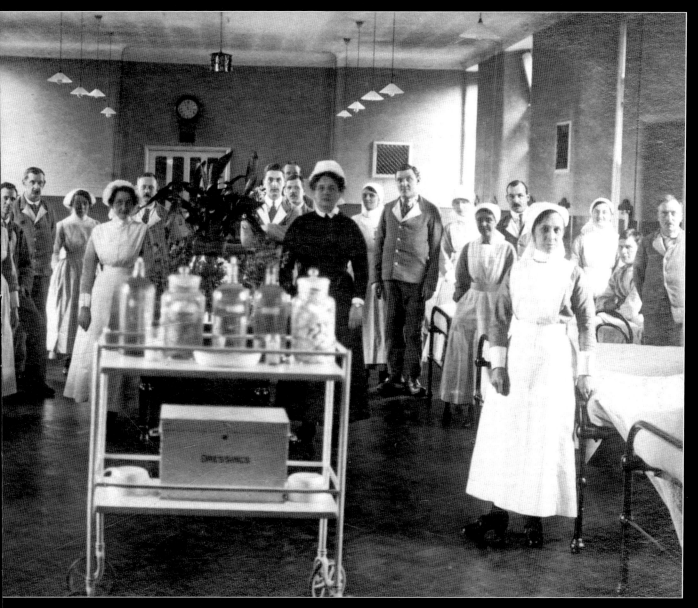

underpowered and carried weak armaments. The much improved Mark III, introduced in March 1942, had great success in the North African campaign, especially at El Alamein.

Above: A number of hospitals had links with the workhouses where the old, poor, insane and destitute were housed in an effort to keep them off the streets and provide them with some form of ordered existence. In return for a roof over their heads, the inmates were expected to work hard for their keep. The County Hospital that opened in 1899 on Park Lodge Road was at the rear of the former workhouse that had been in operation since 1851. This new pavilion plan infirmary was designed by the local architect William Watson and cost £20,000 to build. There were 150 beds and it boasted such modern facilities as filtered air, electric lighting and its very own telephone system. A new

porter's lodge and receiving wards were added at the entrance to the site in 1904. Particular attention was to be given to 'the sick poor of the working class'. During the First World War, Park Lane Auxiliary Hospital was established with 100 beds reserved within the main hospital to treat soldiers injured at the front. Here, these angels of mercy in their starched uniforms gave much needed assistance and reassurance to men whose lives had been blighted by injuries both physical and mental. The workhouse later became known as Stanley View and mainly provided accommodation for the elderly, but also temporary refuges for homeless families and battered wives. The infirmary part was developed as Wakefield County Hospital, becoming part of the National Health Service in 1948. After 1968, it too catered mainly for elderly patients. All the workhouse buildings have now been demolished and the site is occupied by a housing estate.

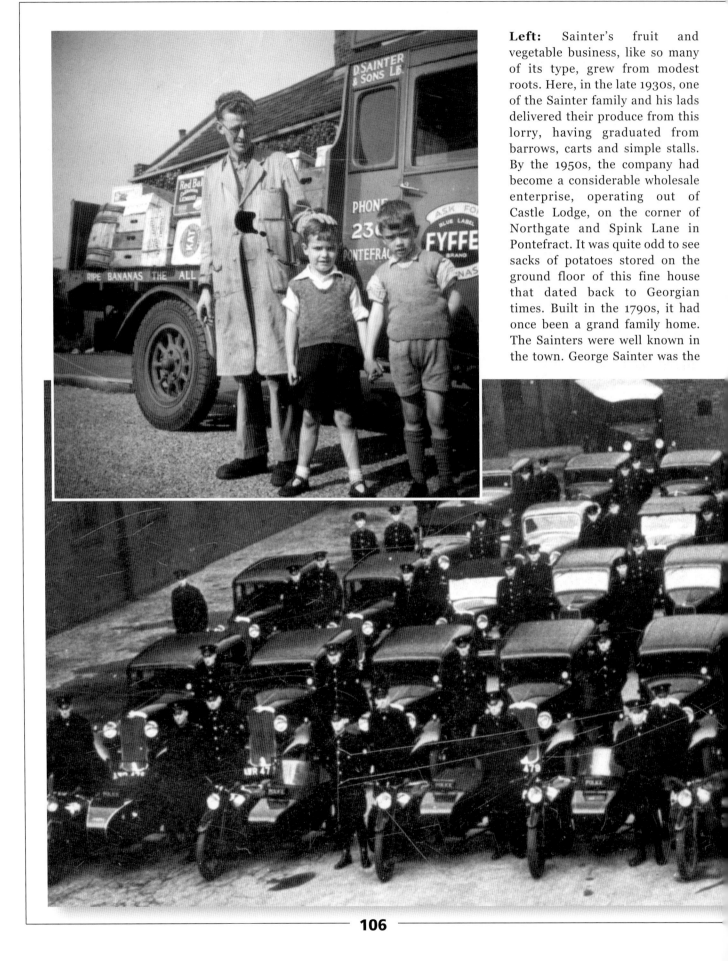

Left: Sainter's fruit and vegetable business, like so many of its type, grew from modest roots. Here, in the late 1930s, one of the Sainter family and his lads delivered their produce from this lorry, having graduated from barrows, carts and simple stalls. By the 1950s, the company had become a considerable wholesale enterprise, operating out of Castle Lodge, on the corner of Northgate and Spink Lane in Pontefract. It was quite odd to see sacks of potatoes stored on the ground floor of this fine house that dated back to Georgian times. Built in the 1790s, it had once been a grand family home. The Sainters were well known in the town. George Sainter was the

Mayor of Pontefract in 1932 and David Sainter held the same office 10 years later. The photograph contains an advertisement for Fyffe's bananas. These would soon disappear from the fruit bowls on the sideboards of our living rooms. 'Yes, we have no bananas', the big hit song of 1923 when sung by Eddie Cantor, was revived with grim irony in the 1940s when we saw not one single hand of this delightful commodity. When the first ones reappeared after the war there was such a rush for them that bananas became as precious as petrol and nylon stockings on the black market.

Below: This was the might of the traffic patrol section of the West Riding Constabulary vehicle fleet. These cars and motorcycle sidecar units were not quite The Sweeney or Starsky and Hutch, but they were the pride of Yorkshire in 1938. Amusingly, we had only just done away with bobbies waving rattles or blowing whistles in efforts to persuade errant motorists to stop. We were now entering a more serious and better organised period of policing, or so we would have if the war had

not intervened. The 1930s had been a problematic decade for road safety. The large increase in the volume of traffic on the road had brought major problems. Road sense for many was minimal. Driving habits were appalling, being selfish and downright dangerous. The roads themselves were not geared up for modern motoring and were better suited to the pony and trap generation than that of Bentleys and even Austin Sevens. Our record for accidents and death was one of the worst in Europe and was a national scandal. The government, for once, grasped the nettle. The provision of electric street lighting was hurried through, as were electrically controlled traffic lights at major junctions. The Highway Code was published, offering sound advice. Halifax's Percy Shaw came up with the simple but lifesaving invention of cats' eyes and Leslie Hore-Belisha promoted the pedestrian crossing. The driving test for all new licence holders became mandatory and our boys in blue were there to provide support and, if necessary, a bit of legal muscle.

Below: Rhubarb, rhubarb. For some reason, this is what actors are supposed to mutter on stage when pretending to hold some form of conversation. Yet, rhubarb is a serious matter, especially if you were Mr Pierce or one of countless other rhubarb farmers who have made this strange vegetable that is eaten as a fruit so popular on

many dinner tables. Rhubarb crumble and custard is the sort of pudding that sends our European neighbours off muttering deep remarks into their frogs' legs or sauerkraut. For a long time, but especially in the middle of the last century, the triangle between Leeds and Wakefield has contained the bulk of the world's supply of this foodstuff. As kiddies we acquired a taste for the bitter-sweet treat by taking pink sticks of the delicious stuff and dipping them in sugar. The flavour was superb, even if it did not do a great deal for the tooth enamel. This cartload was piled high, ready for market. Housewives

knew that it was both cheap and nutritious and the luckiest ones had husbands who also grew well manured crowns of rhubarb on their allotments. Here, many people deliberately force their crop, encouraging early growth by raising the immediate temperature in dark surroundings. This is achieved by such a simple method as placing an upturned bucket over the plant. The same effect is achieved commercially by growing rhubarb in darkened sheds.

Bottom: Photographed in about 1970, this field of rhubarb, growing in the famous triangle just outside Wakefield, actually has its origins in Asia. It was on this continent that the plant was first cultivated and has a long history of use in traditional Chinese medicine. Its introduction to Britain was not recorded until the 17th century. From the late 1870s to the 1950s, trainloads of rhubarb, at 100 tons a time, were carried to Covent Garden Market in London. The industry now runs at a reduced, but still very viable, capacity. Some goes to France as an aid to the production of champagne and it is also used to add flavour to Ruby Gold, a local cheese made from ewes' milk. Youngsters love to play in these fields, using the stalks as makeshift swords and clubs as they act out battles. They must always be careful when they finally decide to scoff their weapons as the leaves contain oxalic acid. This can cause tummy upsets, but you would have to eat about 10 lbs of leaves to suffer any major poisonous backlash.

Cliff School
Providing a First Class Teaching Environment

Home for Wakefield's Cliff Preparatory School is St John's Lodge, Leeds Road. The Cliff Nursery & Pre-Preparatory School is in Bar Lane.

The independent school and nursery take children from 2 to 11 years.

St. John's 'House' was built in 1827 for a cloth merchant, David Smirthwaite, at a cost of about £2,100. It stands at the end of the imposing Georgian terrace of St. John's North, directly opposite St. John's Church.

Smirthwaite almost certainly never lived in the house which was let to Twistleton Haxby, a Wakefield lawyer.

Haxby died in June 1844: his widow gave notice to quit the house in 1845. The building was then occupied by the Reverend Henry Dawson MA, a well-to-do Church of England parson.

From 1886 until 1905 the house was occupied by Samuel Bruce LL.B.JP. The property was then bought by the Wakefield Diocesan Church Organisation Society which installed an assistant for the Lord Bishop of Wakefield whose Palace adjoined the property.

Cliff School was founded in 1939 by Mrs Tattersall: it moved to St. John's Lodge in the late 1940s. Mrs Tattersall's successor, who took over the school in the mid-1960s, bought the building from the Church Commission in 1980.

St. John's Lodge is now a Grade 2 listed building.

In 1987 the school was bought by Mr and Mrs Wallace who developed the site sympathetically, winning a number of architectural, civic and planning awards.

In 2001 the expanding school acquired a building on Bar Lane to house a second nursery and Pre-Prep department.

The following year the school gained the honour of being nominated 'Prep School of the Year' in the Sunday Times after achieving first place in the SATs league tables.

The school was acquired by the prestigious Alpha Plus Group in 2004. Massive financial investment led to the two buildings being extensively refurbished, along with the provision of all the latest technology and teaching aids. A brand new Science Room was opened by Johnny Ball in 2007.

Today the school is looking forward with confidence to another seven decades of providing a first class teaching environment.

*Top left: St John's Lodge. **Bottom left and above:** Pupils rest at playtime and a view inside the nursery in the mid 1990s. **Below:** The Cliff Nursery & Pre-Preparatory School in Bar Lane.*

The Charlesworth Group - Unrivalled Quality and Service

*T*he Charlesworth Group, based in Flanshaw Way Wakefield, is one of the leading UK suppliers of print and publishing services. But it is also a local business with a surprisingly large international presence.

Providing superior quality, cutting-edge typesetting techniques and state-of-the-art digital printing, as well as traditional printing and binding, make up the Group's core activity. Charlesworth however, also offers rights and licensing solutions as well as specialist marketing techniques for the fastest growing market in the world, China.

An extensive client base is made up of universities, not-for-profit organisations, charities, government departments, trade associations and local businesses in the UK as well as global organisations, world leading publishers and learned societies.

From Group headquarters in Wakefield to a wholly-owned subsidiary - Charlesworth China in Beijing - and a North American office in Philadelphia, experienced staff give clients the best possible service by providing tailored solutions to meet their specific requirements.

H. Charlesworth & Co. Ltd was founded by Harry Charlesworth and his wife Olive in 1928. At the outset the company's primary function was the printing of sports-related material; it was based in a small workshop in Huddersfield. A sister company, Hammond Bindery, was established in Wakefield in 1976 located on Flanshaw Way – a site to which the Group headquarters subsequently relocated.

Still family-owned, Charlesworth, has evolved into one of the world's leading providers of typesetting, printing and binding to the learned publishing industry, producing journals, books and other publications both in print and electronically.

Top: Founders, Harry and Olive Charlesworth. **Below:** *A staff outing to Holland in the late 1960s.*

The Group is currently chaired by L Neil Charlesworth, son of the firm's founder. Neil Charlesworth joined the business in the 1950s working for his father as an apprentice. At that time the firm's employees consisted only of Neil and his father along with Neil's mother Olive and his sister Hazel.

During the 1960s the business began to grow, and by 1968 some 30 staff were being employed. Not least amongst those early employees was Walter Firth who would become Managing Director of the Group. Walter had joined the business in 1964 as a manager when the company had a staff of just eight and an annual turnover of a mere £26,000.

Walter became Managing Director in 1988. By the time he retired ten years later the firm had quadrupled in size and achieved annual sales of over £8 million.

A subsidiary company was established in China in May 1999 by the then General Manager, Tao Tao, who today holds the position of Executive Director of Charlesworth China and is assisted

by Xiaoying Chu, Production Director and Amanda Laverick, Chief Operating Officer. Amanda originally worked for Charlesworth in the UK typesetting operation before joining Charlesworth China in 2004.

Charlesworth's Chinese operations have doubled in size over successive years, allowing greatly increased capacity for low cost, high quality typesetting and data services. The wholly-owned subsidiary company Charlesworth (Beijing) Information Services Co Ltd (originally Beijing Charlesworth Software Development Company - BCSD) began trading with just five members of staff. It was formed to provide services which would complement those offered through Charlesworth in the UK. Today CBIS is now more widely known simply as 'Charlesworth China'.

Top left: Computerised typesetting on an IBM in 1973. Above: H. Charlesworth & Co. Ltd's old premises in Huddersfield. Below: A 1970s Charlesworth exhibition stand.

The Chinese company has grown year on year, and expects to continue expanding in the future. The range of services has also developed to become more comprehensive and tailored to the specific needs of clients. All the staff in China are English-speaking graduates with experience of working with English-language publications. Charlesworth China is managed by both English and Chinese staff based in Beijing.

The continued expansion of Charlesworth's Chinese operations meant relocation to new larger premises in Beijing in late 2003, creating further capacity for high quality, low cost typesetting, data capture and conversion services. In addition, the Rights and Licensing team has expanded operations in China, the UK and USA to service growing demand.

Charlesworth China now employs over 200 staff with a second office established just outside Beijing in February 2009.

Back in Britain the Group's core activities focus mainly on providing quality services to publishers. During the summer of 2004 print operations relocated to a more environmentally friendly single-site alongside Hammonds, the Group's Bindery Division in Wakefield, streamlining production in the UK, improving customer service and creating cost efficiencies. The Group continues to offer comprehensive trade binding services through Hammonds.

Group headquarters were also extended and refurbished in 2004, when Charlesworth relocated its printing operations alongside Hammonds. In that same year the Group established a sales office based in Philadelphia, USA, promoting services offered through Charlesworth China. In 2006 this became a distinct corporate entity

Top left: At the 1985 Litho Week Awards The Charlesworth Group were outright winners of the Monotype Award for Scientific and Technical Composition - Neil Charlesworth receives the trophy from the Chairman of Monotype International. *Above:* Former Sales Director, Graham Laycock, alongside the newly installed Heidelberg press in the late 1980s. *Below:* New machinery bought by Hammond Bindery in the 1980s to provide quality finishing at realistic prices.

and the British National Export Council. The group visited New York, Boston and Chicago in search of sales. Key to the company's ever increasing confidence at that time was investment in state-of-the-art printing technology.

In 1999 Charlesworth won The Queen's Award for Export Achievement.

Printing has been around for over 500 years. In the mid 15th century, Johannes Gutenberg in Germany invented movable type. William Caxton set up England's first printing press to use moveable type at Westminster in 1476 and the first book

under the name *The Charlesworth Group (USA), Inc.* *The Charlesworth Group's* US Office was established to service the Group's growing list of US based clients. Offices situated between Washington DC and New York, in Philadelphia provide an ideal location. The US office provides a vital 'real time' contact point for customers and promotes the benefits of the Charlesworth China operations to a wide range of US publishers. The Chief Executive Officer of *The Charlesworth Group (USA), Inc.* is Adrian Stanley. Adrian was previously Production Director of Charlesworth China (then known as BCSD) where he was instrumental in the successful growth of the business there. The Group's interest in the US market began nearly 40 years before the establishment of a permanent presence in America. It was in 1968 Neil Charlesworth first flew to the USA to seek out new sales opportunities as a member of an export mission organised by the British Federation of Master Printers

Top and above left: *Hammond Bindery, Flanshaw Way, Wakefield, pictured shortly after its official opening in 1985.*
Below: *A new Freccia automatic sewing machine in 1993.*

subsequently pay enormous dividends, ensuring that Charlesworth's was always at the forefront of every new opportunity in a rapidly evolving industry.

In Wakefield continuous investment means the Group's press room and bindery remain equipped with the very latest machinery to deliver rapid turnaround yet still providing the best possible quality and most environmentally friendly output at competitive prices. To maintain its position within an elite group of just a handful of British printers Charlesworth has married all the traditional craft skills of the printer's art to the most powerful of today's computer technology. The process of typesetting by computer is continuously refined – not only in terms of sophisticated hardware but

known to have been issued there by him was an edition of Chaucer's Canterbury Tales. Until the 1960s, however, the basic idea behind printing and printing presses had remained essentially the same, despite such technical advances as the invention of the rotary printing press in 1847. But in the 1960s a revolution in printing technology was about to burst on the printing industry – the computer. And one of the firm's eager to be at the leading edge of modern technology would be H. Charlesworth & Co Ltd. The acquisition of one of the first IBM machines to be used in the UK printing industry by the company saw the beginnings of a completely new form of typesetting service, and a crucial switch from hot metal to the lithographic printing process.

Typesetting capacity built up dramatically as markets developed in the academic field for technical and complex typesetting. By 1978 the firm decided to offer an alternative typesetting system to the already existing IBM strike-on composition. A Monophoto 1000 system consisting of six input keyboards and two Monophoto 4000/8 output devices were bought.

Early investment in word processing, laser technology and the very latest in typesetting equipment would

Top left: Former Managing Director, Walter Firth, retires in 1998. Neil and Hazel Charlesworth present Walter with some gifts on behalf of the company. ***Above:*** *The Beijing building which is home to Charlesworth China.* ***Far left:*** *left to right: Xiaoying Chu, China Production Director, Adrian Stanley, Chief Executive Officer of The Charlesworth Group (USA), Inc. and Tao Tao, Executive Director of Charlesworth China.* ***Left:*** *Amanda Laverick, Chief Operating Officer, Charlesworth China.*

also with innovative software developed in-house to meet the unique needs of each of Charlesworth's varied and demanding clients. Integrated management information systems give managers and supervisors full control over day to day operations whilst allowing customer service teams access to timely and accurate production information.

Since co-location in 2004 the Group has implemented lean manufacturing techniques and achieved both ISO 9001 quality management accreditation and ISO 14001

environmental accreditation. The Group is now concentrating on another key priority, gaining FSC certification, developing further the high environmental standards Charlesworth sets itself.

In 2006 David Boothman became Managing Director of Charlesworth. David had previously held the positions of head of the Bindery division and after co-location, Production Director. Also that year Charlesworth achieved ISO 9001 accreditation for both its UK and Beijing operations, demonstrating the Group's continued commitment to quality on an international scale.

Today Wakefield's Charlesworth Group is looking better than ever, offering a wide range of solutions to publishers - from typesetting and print to the sale of rights. The hundred strong local workforce, many of whom have been with the company for over 25 years, together with the Charlesworth family, can take justifiable pride in a business whose vision is unbounded.

Top left, above left and above right: *Views inside Charlesworth's Flanshaw Way facility.* ***Left:*** *Managing Director, David Boothman.* ***Right:*** *Executive Chairman, Neil Charlesworth.*

Harlow & Milner - Firm Foundations
Proudly based in the Wakefield area for over 70 years

The building firm of Harlow and Milner Ltd came perilously close to never happening at all. Yet since its formation in 1937 Harlow & Milner Ltd, based on Milner Way, Ossett, has become established as one of the leading building contractors in West Yorkshire. The firm has earned an impressive reputation for reliability and technical expertise in the construction of residential, commercial and industrial properties of every type.

Founded by Bernard Harlow and Raymond Milner, Harlow & Milner Ltd quickly established itself as a reliable and honest contractor. Early expertise was generally within the new build housing sector. During the war years of 1939 to 1945 a speciality developed in bomb-damage-repairs on all types of structures, including a dedicated team based in London.

The first time Bernard Harlow, a southerner from the Isle of Wight, approached Raymond Milner, a bricklayer from Dewsbury to discuss a partnership he was told "Sorry, not now. Come back after working hours."

Raymond Milner later explained "I was not allowed to spend my work time chatting to other people. I was paid to work – and I had to."

But in 1937 the partnership did get off the ground.

That the business should not only get off the ground, but actually thrive, is, in retrospect, quite remarkable. The 'hungry thirties' was perhaps the least auspicious decade of the entire 20th

Above: Raymond and Catherine Milner. **Below:** *Harlow & Milner's Kettlethorpe Estate, Wakefield, scheme in 1953.*

The small firm couldn't afford to put up with idlers, and only half-jokingly became known as 'Harlow and Kill'Em'. But one of the firm's founding first principles was to give a fair day's pay for a fair day's work.

The partnership got its first contract because the local council wanted to give the complete contract to a single firm instead of splitting it up into individual trades as it had done in the past. The contract for a whole group of 14 houses however, was for only £4,000, with £200 extra because Harlow & Milner were doing the whole job. The duo of Raymond and Bernard succeeded in not only in making the job pay but also finished it on time, ensuring that the council was thoroughly satisfied with the work.

As the country went to war in 1939, building all but stopped, however, as the firm was working on a few houses, it was allowed to finish them because they had got past laying the damp-proof course.

century to think of starting a new business venture. Millions were unemployed. And those who were in work had little money to spare.

Many folk from the north of England set off south in search of work. Almost unbelievably for the times Bernard Harlow had taken the opposite tack, actually coming to the north from the south of England in search of employment.

Harlow & Milner were however, kept busy during the war years working for the Army, Navy and Air Ministries and this was not all that had to be done, when bombs started falling on London the Government made it clear to the building trade that if volunteers did not travel to London to repair the damage it would commandeer men to do the work.

Bernard had come to Dewsbury looking for work. It was there that he found himself a partner in bricklayer Raymond Milner who was working on Dewsbury's Wheelwright Grammar School.

At first the new business was on a rather precarious footing. Raymond Milner put up his share of the necessary cash with the help of his sisters; "We bought a wheelbarrow, picks and shovels and began work" he later recalled. "I had no money at all then – I was just a journeyman bricklayer, but my sisters helped me find £200 and we began work on a local authority housing contract at Thornhill near Dewsbury."

*Top left: Chickenley Estate, scheme in 1953. **Above:** Part of the main building yard, joinery and concrete shops in 1978. **Below:** Harlow & Milner's headquarters and administrative centre, Milner Way, 1978.*

Bernard volunteered to take a party of two or three men from each local firm down. But after a while he could not cope with the constant travelling and Raymond took over that side of the business. Whilst he was away, Raymond's wife Catherine helped with the running of the business which at that time, was still based in Dewsbury.

After the war ended in 1945 things started moving once again. The firm tendered to build the temporary houses that local authorities were now putting up. After three attempts Harlow & Milner got a contract in Dewsbury, they were also successful in securing projects to build temporary houses in Halifax and Ossett.

When permanent houses could be built again the firm came up against an unexpected problem. Many bricklayers had become used to a different environment whilst working for the Government during the war. The Government had paid a bonus after a man had laid 40 bricks per hour. Before the war bricklayers were expected to be able to lay 70 bricks an hour as a matter of course.

In 1950 Bernard decided that life in the north of England was not for him and retired, leaving Raymond Milner to run the business single handedly. This he did with some gusto, the company flourishing under his sole stewardship, it focused on building high quality social housing, winning over 30 awards for excellence in construction. These family homes are the council houses that many thousands of the readers of this publication live in today. In 1967 when at the age of 67, he handed over control to his sons Frank and John.

The third brother Edward, who had become a dairy farmer, also became a Director two years later, when his farm became integrated into the business to allow for further investment in both farming and construction.

Raymond did not sit back and take life easy even after handing over control to his sons. He still continued taking a very active interest in running the firm until 1972 when illness forced him to take three months off.

"They reckoned that if they could manage without me for three months they could manage without me altogether. Since then I think they've asked me for advice twice and ignored it both times" he would later recall.

*Above: John Milner (left), Frank Milner (centre) and Edward Milner. **Below:** Staff members pictured in 1987, left to right: Roy Collis, Stuart Leech, Vera Wimpenny, John Milner and Brian Denham. Mr Collis retired the following year having been with H&M for forty years.*

Following the 1979 governmental change in policy for housing provision (the cessation of new build council houses), councils virtually ceased house building. The company began looking for other work to fill the gap and turned its hand to projects such as sports facilities like the Lightwaves centre in central Wakefield. The firm also sought out and nurtured other successful partnerships, working more and more closely with many of the newly formed housing associations and developing an expertise in industrial and commercial construction, which added yet another string to its already impressive bow.

The firm would build many local factory, warehouse and office units. The biggest departure from previous work however, was to set up a small works department to look after low value projects and maintenance contracts.

affordable housing, whilst at the same time continuing to deliver bespoke construction projects in the commercial, industrial, health and education sectors.

Since being founded in 1937 the firm has come a long way. In the 1930s it had employed just 12 men. At the peak they employed 300. But the introduction of machinery had revolutionised the construction industry making redundant the armies of labourers that were once a common sight. By the mid-1970s Harlow & Milner was employing around 200 people. A level which was maintained up to the recent separation of Milnerbuild Ltd and today Harlow & Milner employs around 100 dedicated professional staff.

The recession of the 1980s brought with it difficult trading conditions made even more challenging by the de-merger of the company to allow the three brothers to focus their talents on their own individual areas of expertise. More recently, a period of growth, spearheaded by Richard Milner, allowed the company to perform a management buy in to the repairs and maintenance division of the company, which traded as Milnerbuild, bringing in two new partners, separating the two divisions of the business and creating Milnerbuild Ltd which has subsequently relocated to Neo Court, Cross Green, Leeds, where it continues to thrive and grow despite the current difficult trading conditions within the industry.

Milnerbuild Ltd now operates solely as a repairs, maintenance and refurbishment company for local authority and housing association clients. Harlow & Milner continues to work with local authorities, private developers and housing associations delivering high quality,

Above left: *Marsh Way Sports Centre, Wakefield, known locally as lightwaves a H&M prestige development in the 1980s.* **Top right:** *The Esther Grove, Lupset, housing development.* **Below:** *Ossett Police Station, built in the mid-1980s and one of the first purpose-built task force headquarters, it has, however, never been used as such.*

each day. A practice continued by his two sons John and Frank and continued to this day by his grandson Richard.

The family atmosphere has changed little down the years although the bricks and mortar surrounding it have. The firm is now based at Trident House on Milner Way, having moved there in 2008, the de-merger of Milnerbuild Ltd to Leeds meant that its then headquarters in Milner House were no longer suitable. This evolution had happened twice before when the company moved from its first yard in Dewsbury, and then the later one in Warrengate, Wakefield, which gave way to the city's inner ring road, Marsh Way.

One of the key ingredients of long-term progress had been the loyalty of Harlow & Milner's staff. Over 70 employees have been awarded 25 years service gold watches – something quite unique in the industry. Many of these men have worked for the company for 30 and even 40 years. One who stands out above all is bricklayer Stuart Bromby who on retirement in 2009 had completed an extraordinary 50 years unbroken service with the firm. Stuart started work as an apprentice bricklayer just after his 15th birthday in 1959, winning a silver trowel for excellence in 1965 (one of only 5 awarded nationally and in an era when apprenticeships were much more commonplace). Had he just walled bricks in his time with the company and not stone and other materials, it is estimated that he would have laid in excess of 10,000,000 bricks, quite a feat.

Raymond Milner always set an example to the workforce by making sure he was always first there and last to go home

John retired in 1999 at the age of 60, selling his interest in the business to his son Richard who a little earlier had become the firm's Managing Director. Richard's brother Andrew rejoined to the company in 2003, his expertise lies in sales and marketing which will help the company as it moves forward through the current, troubled, economic times.

Harlow & Milner Ltd is dedicated solely to the construction industry. Its primary function is that of main building contractors, specialising in social housing, private housing, health, education,

Top left: A view inside Milner Joinery.
Above: Four generations of the Milner family: Raymond (left) John (right) Richard (centre) and eldest son Luke at his christening in 1989, the first photograph ever taken of 4 generations of the family. Left: Castle Road, built in 2006 and at the time an extremely contentious development with local residents but now considered to be one of the finest examples of urban regeneration in the local area.

Hall Residential Care Home, Leeds. The project will cost excess of £3.4 million – almost a thousand times more than the firm's very first contract back in 1937. The company is also yet again involved in changing the skyline of Wakefield with the construction of the landmark building opposite Westgate train station (pictured above), the mixed use development of residential and commercial units was completed in late 2009.

Despite the many changes down the years, not least in the scale of projects undertaken, there is still a feeling within Harlow & Milner Ltd of belonging to a family firm, a feeling strengthened by the fact that the third generation of the Milner family is at the helm driving their grandfather's heritage forward in the 21st century.

commercial developments and mixed use developments. The diversification gives it practical in-depth knowledge of legislation such as: SDS - Scheme Design Standards, Code for sustainable homes - Working with our Environment, Secured by Design - Peace of mind for our community and Local Labour Initiative - Integration of our business and the community we work in.

That diversity of service provision has been maintained since Richard Milner took hold of the reins in 1999, bringing with him new energy for the challenge of the new century employment and working practices, whilst further developing the quality and reliability foundations laid over the previous two generations.

More recent history has included greater community integration and local labour initiatives that have further reinforced the firm's reputation within the industry and connected markets.

The company is now ideally placed to embrace the new challenges of the 21st century and is keen to continue its evolution and development with new partners and communities.

Amongst Harlow & Milner's latest projects is work on an exciting four storey extension of a Headingley

Top left: *Harlow & Milner completing the redevelopment of 117 Westgate, Wakefield, in July 2009.* **Left:** *Current Harlow & Milner Managing Director, Richard Milner.* **Below:** *The current team: Julie Barrett (Buyer and accounts), Darren Gill (Health & Safety), Graeme Pearce (Chief Estimator), Andrew Shaw (Chief Quantity Surveyor), John Allsop (Contracts Director) and Richard Milner (Managing Director).*

Eric France Scrap Metal Merchants
Experts in Delivering Total Metal Solutions.

When Eric France left the armed forces after serving in the Far East, it was inevitable that he would 'forge' a career in the world of metal. From his experience working with primary ingots, global metal trading and scrap he had an encyclopaedic practical knowledge of almost every aspect of metal.

He became General Manager of a local lead works before accepting the role of MD designate at G. B. Housley, scrap metal merchants, continuing to gain more expertise in metal. Unexpectedly, redundancy from this company in 1976 gave the ambitious Eric an opportunity to establish his own company.

Later, in 1976, Eric began trading as Eric France Metal from premises in Ings Mills, off Dale Street in Ossett, West Yorkshire. The premises were not ideal. Working in what is now part of the Victorian Bathrooms showrooms, somehow, he put up with the lack of electricity, a leaking roof and countless other difficulties in what can only be described as truly grim conditions. Despite this wholly discouraging environment, Eric set about the uphill task of building a scrap and metal trading business from scratch. To his networking skills, his in-depth knowledge of the metals industry and his acute and instinctive business skills, Eric contributed his honest, hard graft.

The business grew quickly and after only one year, Eric began the search for more suitable and appropriate premises for his rapidly growing business. A former rag grinder's mill and wartime ambulance station in Church Street, a matter of yards from his first address, provided the ideal solution. Walter Benson and Son, an existing scrap metal business, initially on the site at Embassy Works, agreed after relatively brief negotiations to sell the business and the premises,

Embassy Works, to Eric. In mid-1977, Embassy Works became the new home of Eric France Metals. With the new and improved premises generating an added enthusiasm and the continued rise in the value of non-ferrous metals, the business continued to grow in strength. Now employing a small and dedicated team, the company operated scrap trade through the yard and increased its skip collection service from engineering firms, factories and other merchants. By this time, the company's skip and flat-bed wagons operated a scrap collection service from as far as Birmingham to the south up to Newcastle in the north.

Around the same time, in the mid-1980s, one employee, in particular, caught the attention for his school holiday exploits on the yard forklift. This was Jonathan France, Eric's son, who had clearly inherited his father's passion for metal and was already proving an expert in grading, pricing and dealing scrap metal. However, his main area of interest was the global trading of large amounts of metal on the London Metal Exchange. Since his days in the lead industry, Eric had traded metal internationally and Jonathan had shown himself to be more than a willing student displaying great promise. At the time Jonathan left school, he had already become an integral part of the success of the business. He had secured a motor racing scholarship and left the family business for university. However, after less than a year into his further education Jonathan could not resist the temptation to return to the family metals business and joined the rest of the team at Embassy Works as a full time scrap man. Without enjoying any special treatment, Jonathan swiftly settled into a junior role in the business which involved everything from driving the wagons to sweeping the floors.

Exhibiting a natural instinct for the business, Jonathan quickly gained the respect of colleagues as he learned the ropes and began to take a more influential role in the business and was made responsible for updating machinery and for

bringing more modern and cost-effective practices into the yard. By the mid-1990s, having served his

Top left: Founder, Eric France. **Far left:** *Eric at work in the 1980s.* **Above and below:** *Staff grading metal inside Embassy Works in the late 1980s and early 1990s.*

apprenticeship, Jonathan was ready to take control of the business. These proved to be auspicious times for the business, as the global requirement for primary metals hit a new high with furious trading on the London Metal Exchange. Simultaneously, the growth of the internet and on-line trading also allowed for an unprecedented increase in trading opportunities. Without hesitation, Jonathan embraced the new technology and the global market whilst maintaining a close eye on scrap going through the yard.

This period saw unprecedented growth for the company. The Eric France global trading portfolio has continued to grow and the business has become increasingly successful. A measure of the growth of the business is that in 1998 the company had a turnover of over £300,000, which, ten years later, in 2008, had risen to over £300 million! In 2000, Eric decided to retire from the business which he had first set up 24 years previously. Having enjoyed remarkable success in the global commodities market, Jonathan decided, in 2004, to focus on increasing the footfall through the yard, where, by this time, trade had reached a plateau. Recognising the need to introduce new advertising, marketing and communication techniques, Jonathan looked to the highly competitive high street retail sector for inspiration and his determination to follow his own judgement and experience as opposed to employing expensive research agencies was thoroughly vindicated with a ten-fold increase in business as a result of a powerful series of advertising campaigns. As one of the most recognisable brands in the region, Eric France Metals,

through sometimes controversial advertising, has earned a reputation amongst the experts for creating one of the most sophisticated and successful communication campaigns ever seen in West Yorkshire.

The 2008 banking crisis, together with a world recession also affecting the scrap industry and the global metal trade, has required the company and the industry to make some tough decisions. However, through careful planning, management and

Top left: *Eric and Jonathan France pictured during Jonathan's early years at Eric France Metals.* ***Bottom left:*** *Jonathan takes delivery of their first baling machine in 1990.* ***Above:*** *Eric and Jonathan alongside one of the company's skip wagons, 1990s.* ***Left:*** *An aerial view of Embassy Works, Church Street, in 2002.*

sensible investment, the Ossett based scrap yard has been able to turn difficult times into new opportunities and continues to lead the way in these uncertain times.

With over 100 years combined experience in the team, Eric France Metals has continued to pioneer new and innovative ways of working and sought out new directions in which to take the company. As a family owned business, the company retains a firm grasp on the concept of value and service excellence for its customers. A blend of professional determination, high standards and the personal integrity has enabled the company to retain its place at the forefront of all its activities in the metal trade.

The Group's dedication to providing added value systems such as fully traceable transactions, real-time prices from the London Metal Exchange, prompt payment terms and a dedicated fleet of appropriate vehicles, has ensured an all-embracing service provision to all its trade customers. The emphasis on the supply of high quality grade metals and supplies to industries throughout the world has ensured a secure and developing reputation.

The company's ability to embrace the requirements of newer industries, such as electronics, has made the company less dependent on individual areas of activity.

With an innovative and progressive owner at its helm, Eric France Metals has never been afraid to look forwards. Focusing on providing

a range of continually evolving and relevant services, the business has always identified new new methods of operation, delivered unexpected niche services and kept the needs of the customer at the forefront of the operation.

Above: *Embassy Racing's first WF01 car as a constructor.*
Below: *Staff pose for a photograph with the Rugby League Challenge Cup.*

Having gained a motor racing scholarship in his teens, largely through his interest in engineering, Jonathan's love affair with motorsport saw him found his very own Embassy Racing team, in 2003.

In 2005, he turned the racing team into a wholly owned in-house motorsports team, establishing a headquarters and engineering premises in West Yorkshire, employing a full-time race engineer, mechanics and support staff. The team's involvement in the 2007 Le Mans series saw it competing against the big factory teams, such as Audi, Peügeot and Aston Martin. In 2008, Embassy Racing became a constructor, developing two WF01's to run in the Le Mans Series as well as two Triumph Daytona 675 bikes to run in the British Supersport Championship.

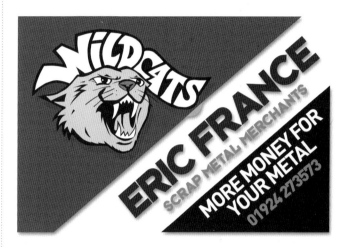

An attractive bonus for customers is the knowledge that Eric France Metals takes its environmental responsibilities very seriously, cognisant of the need, at all times, to protect and preserve the earth's finite natural resources. As a major, successful family-run business, Eric France Metals has demonstrated its commitment to its community through sponsorship and since 2006 has been the main sponsor for Wakefield Wildcats Rugby League Team. The company has also provided sponsorship for West Yorkshire Rugby League team Dewsbury Rams.

Above left: *Wakefield Trinity players pay a visit to Eric France's Embassy Works, pictured are: Danny Brough with the Challenge Cup, Jamie Rooney in the centre and captain, Jason Demetriou.* **Above:** *A Wakefield Wildcats flag.* **Below:** *A Christmas greeting card from the team at Eric France Metals.*

Joseph Rhodes - The Spirit of Innovation Lives On

Today Wakefield-based Group Rhodes is one of Europe's largest Original Equipment Manufacturers in its field, supplying a wide range of machinery for metalforming, material handling, clay preparation, concrete working and special purpose applications. The Group also specialises in the design, manufacture and commissioning of technical fabrications and structural assemblies for the Offshore Oil and Gas industry.

Group companies manufacture and market over fifty basic product ranges, and justifiable pride is taken in the ability to design, develop and manufacture bespoke machinery and complete turnkey solutions. The Group regularly exports around one third of its output to over thirty countries and operates from an eight-acre site at Belle Vue, Wakefield, with over 15,000 sq. metres of factory space.

The main divisions of the Group consist of Joseph Rhodes, Craven Fawcett, Beauford Engineers and Rhodes Interform.

It was in 1824 that Joseph Rhodes, a young engineer, designed and built his first machine in a workshop in Wakefield. At the time Wakefield was a small place with a population of barely twelve thousand and a trade based on wool and corn. It was, however, close to the South Yorkshire coalfields and the growing iron and steel industry of Sheffield, both of which provided the expanding business with the necessary resources to manufacture new and innovative products.

The 19th century saw the invention of a great variety of Rhodes' sheet metal working machines which helped so much to bring cheap metalware into ordinary domestic use. A Joseph Rhodes catalogue from 1895 stresses the value of Rhodes' presses in making tins, oil cans and brass goods for the home.

In the second half of the 19th century Joseph Rhodes' two sons, William and George joined the firm. The business had moved to new premises in Ings Road, Wakefield which Joseph named the 'Grove Iron Works'. A period of expansion followed with the firm, now Joseph Rhodes & Sons, winning medals at world fairs and exhibitions for products as varied as jewellers' rolling machines and can-making machinery.

Joseph gradually retired from the business in order to give more time to municipal affairs. Although he came from a staunch Tory family, he had entered the Town Council as a Liberal and was appointed an Alderman. On 11th November 1865 he was elected Mayor of Wakefield and later served as a Justice of the Peace and a member of the Council before his death in July, 1876, at the age of 72.

Joseph Rhodes & Sons became a limited company in 1899 and registered 'The Colossus of Rhodes' as its trade mark. William and George Rhodes managed the firm jointly until 1900 when George left to set up his own business.

William Rhodes not only showed a keen desire to promote the family firm but also, like his father, entered local politics. In 1894 he became a Councillor. William was elected Mayor of Wakefield on 9th November, 1903, but died in office the following year.

Charles Rhodes, William's son, in turn took his place at the head of the company - the third Rhodes in a direct line to head the business. Under Charles, and his Managing Director Harry Ridgway, the company developed machines to meet the Government requirements of two world wars.

Harry Ridgway, who had been appointed Chief Draughtsman in 1918 at the remarkably young age of 21, presided over the design of presses for purposes ranging from the manufacture of petrol cans and aircraft components to compressing explosive charges into shells.

In 1921 the company moved from The Ings to its present site at Belle Vue. Employment at the company had grown to the extent that the move forced several public houses in The Ings area to close, including the Ings Tavern which had served Rhodes' personnel for several decades.

During the Second World War, Rhodes presses were sent overseas to India, Africa and the Middle East. Desert workshops were using Rhodes presses during Montgomery's

*Top left: Founder, Joseph Rhodes. **Bottom left and above:** Views inside the Ings Road factory, circa 1904. **Below:** The fitting shop at Belle Vue in the mid-1930s.*

North African campaign, whilst in both world wars Royal Navy warships were fitted with sheet metal shops in which Rhodes folding machines, shears and bending rollers were installed.

The company had entered the export market early in its history, opening an office in Paris as early as 1910, but exports increased sharply after the Second World War particularly to Europe and the USA. In the 1950s that export drive was assisted by Harry Ridgway's invention of the world's first hydraulic shear and press brake, patented in 1943.

A series of innovative products rapidly followed the introduction of the hydraulic shear, amongst which the

stagger feed press, for the production of such tin plate items as canister lids and shoe polish tins. An impact extrusion press used in the forming of battery casings and toothpaste tubes, proved particularly successful.

By the mid-1950s the company could boast a product range of over 1,000 types of machines for the sheet metal working industry. The British Machine Tool Engineering Magazine for March 1954 reported such a range to be "the largest variety made by any firm in the world".

In 1959 the Rhodes family's control of the company came to an end. Charles Rhodes died, still holding a large number of the company's shares, and although Charles' son Stanley joined the business for a short period of time, the company had to be sold to pay the excessive 'death duty' tax.

In 1961 Joseph Rhodes was acquired by Lindustries, a company which was diversifying into engineering from a textile base. Continuity of Rhodes management was however, ensured through Harry Ridgway J.P. He continued to guide the company until his retirement in 1968 after 58 years with the firm.

Lindustries, under whose ownership the company had prospered, was itself the subject of a successful take-over bid

Top left: *The machine assembly room in 1954.* **Left:** *Assembling a double action mechanical press in the early 1950s.* **Above:** *A bird's eye view of the Joseph Rhodes premises in 1996.*

by Hanson Trust plc in 1979. Joseph Rhodes Limited became part of an enlarged Hanson group, dropping the '& Sons' from the company name.

However, the recession of the early 1980s diminished the returns generated by the company and in 1984 the Hanson Board agreed to a Management Buy-Out by the Commercial Director, Ian Ridgway, son of Harry Ridgway, and by Production Director, John Blacker.

Under private ownership once again after an intervening period of 23 years the company was flexible enough to re-focus on the design of high technology products yet at the same time repay the financial support provided to the Management Buy-Out team by Yorkshire Enterprise and the Wakefield Council.

In 1994 John Blacker retired, returning the now 170 year old company to a family business headed by Chairman and Managing Director, Ian Ridgway.

The new management team made several acquisitions of synergistic metalforming companies in the mid-1990s. HME, Bentley, Dualform and a software house were purchased to add to Cowlishaw Walker, an acquisition that had already been made under the Lindustries Group.

'Group Rhodes' came into being in 2001 as a result of the acquisition of Craven Fawcett. Established in 1843, Craven Fawcett was a pioneer in the field of Clayworking machinery.

The 'Craven' side of the business was founded by William Craven and Richard Bradley, two young engineers who produced revolutionary machinery for automating the production of bricks. By 1853 the company's Stiff Plastic Brickmaking Machines were being sold throughout the UK and to many oversees markets, including South Africa, Germany and Australia. In 1972 Bradley and Craven pooled their resources with rival Leeds firm, Thomas C. Fawcett.

In 2003 Group Rhodes purchased a division of engineering companies from Motherwell Bridge Plc, which it renamed Rhodes Interform Limited. Today Rhodes Interform designs and manufactures special purpose built presses and machinery. Subsidiary companies include the international names of Fielding and Platt, Chester Hydraulics, John Shaw, Henry Berry, Beauford Engineers and Berry Refractories.

Geared towards efficient and effective production, the Interform standard range of machinery is utilised throughout manufacturing industry, from the nuclear and pharmaceutical sectors through to plastics and textiles. Rhodes Interform also provides complete turnkey solutions for specialised machinery, particularly for high technology applications within the Aerospace industry.

More recent additions to Group Rhodes include Beauford Engineers, originally based in Eland, West Yorkshire, but re-launched in 2005 as a supplier of equipment for deep sea oil and gas exploration. Technology from this business, combined with that from the Group's aerospace division was used in 2009 to launch Rhodes Environmental, a provider of processing technology to the waste management industry.

Although today the product range, methods of production and markets serviced have changed enormously since 1824, Group Rhodes remains proud of the fact that it nurtures a dedicated workforce in a traditional yet dynamic manufacturing environment. The development of skills, training and vocational qualifications are an essential part of the Group's policy for future growth and the need to meet the challenging demands of an ever-changing marketplace.

Above: A view over the factory floor in the mid-1990s.
Below: A 2009 view of A Rhodes Hot Forming Press undergoing trials prior to dispatch.

Silcoates School - A Light Forged in Fire

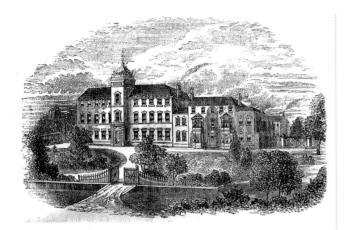

'Clarior ex Ignibus'. For most Silcoates students this Latin inscription is simply the motto that can be read beneath the school's badge, a central feature of which is a phoenix. The legendary phoenix was a bird which was said to burst into flame only to be reborn from its own ashes. Silcoates' motto is in fact a reminder of the rebirth of the present school after its predecessor had been destroyed by fire in 1904 - and to the indomitable spirit of the founders in rebuilding from the ashes. Today the Silcoates School Foundation consists of three schools: Silcoates School, for boys and girls aged from 7 to 18 (the Junior School from 7-11 and Senior School from 11-18) on one self-contained site in Wrenthorpe, near Wakefield. Just down the road from Silcoates School, Sunny Hill House School caters for boys and girls from 3-7, whilst housed in a former convent at Horbury, just four miles from Silcoates, St. Hilda's School educates boys from 0-7 and girls from 0-11.

The first school was founded in 1820 by a handful of Congregationalists who, with the example before them of a Lewisham school for non-conformists, decided there was a place for a similar school in the north. Silcoates Hall was bought from the Lumb family and The Yorkshire Dissenters' Grammar School opened its doors. The next few years, however, saw only struggle and frustration: although in theory the Congregationalists wanted their school they were slow to support it and in the short space of ten years it was forced to close. Its successor, a grammar school and commercial academy, also failed through lack of support.

Though some of the promoters had suffered heavy monetary losses they nevertheless were determined to try again. A third venture was promoted, this time for the

*Top left: Silcoates School from an advert in 1879. **Above:** Pupil William Foster's school book dated January, 1846. **Below left:** A class donning mortar boards pose for a photograph in 1885. **Below:** The school football team in 1898-1899.*

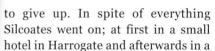

sons of non-conformist ministers in the York and Lancaster dioceses. By the end of the first year there were only twenty two pupils, though the numbers rose to thirty six when the sons of ministers were admitted from other counties, and also the sons of missionaries. At Silcoates Hall, now leased to the school, the Headmaster and his one assistant taught the boys in a schoolroom above the coachman's house, an old building which is still in existence. But only when the sons of laymen were also permitted to attend in 1842 did Silcoates begin to pay its way. Despite a few uncertain years, with the appointment of Dr Bewglass as Headmaster the school began to develop, though financially its future continued to be precarious. More trouble lay in store. The lease of Silcoates Hall was almost at an end and the owner decided to sell. The Governors were faced with three possible decisions - to close the school, acquire another site, or buy the estate. After much deliberation they decided to buy; a bold step, for the price was £15,000. However, with little difficulty the purchase money was raised and in 1871 a new and enlarged Silcoates was opened with fifty pupils. It seemed as if at last prosperity was within sight. But troubles had not been left behind and the greatest disaster of all came in 1904. Silcoates was almost wholly destroyed by fire during the Easter holidays. Yet out of tragedy was produced the nucleus of today's splendid school. The Committee, the Trustees and, most of all, the Headmaster, Mr J A Yonge, refused

to give up. In spite of everything Silcoates went on; at first in a small hotel in Harrogate and afterwards in a house in Saltburn. No school, however, could flourish for long in temporary quarters. To rebuild would cost at least £10,000 if, as was envisaged, Silcoates was to remain independent. Three foundation stones were laid on 2nd November, 1907; one for Yorkshire, one for Lancashire, and one on behalf of the Trustees. In October, 1908 Silcoates began life once more, this time with dormitory accommodation for a hundred boys. It was a brand new school except for the original Silcoates Hall which, the only part to survive the fire, became the headmaster's house. The new school had laboratories and music rooms, a gymnasium, assembly hall and large covered playground, besides the usual form rooms, dining room and kitchen. Later, a swimming bath was given by the Old Boys. In 1947, when Sub Lieutenant James Robert Fowler

Silcoates School, NEAR WAKEFIELD.

Opening of the New Buildings, 1st OCTOBER, 1908.

Top left: *The school ablaze in the fire of 1904.* **Top right:** *The headmaster's house was the only part of the school to survive the fire.* **Far left:** *Pupils pictured during the spell at Saltburn.* **Above:** *The opening of the new buildings in October, 1908.* **Left:** *The opening ceremony of the school chapel in 1928.*

a specialist geography room and library for the seniors (the existing library being handed over to the juniors).

There were new tennis courts, too, and a new cricket field where Wilfred Rhodes, then seventy-one years old, bowled the first over to Brian Sellars. In Wrenthorpe a nearby house was bought to accommodate another twenty

Hodgson, R.N., died whilst helping to rescue Jewish immigrants off Haifa, his parents gave his estate to the school to equip and maintain a science library. However, a school is about more than just buildings. Mr Sydney Moore became Headmaster in 1918. His twenty five years of outstanding leadership added immeasurably to the academic and spiritual progress of the school. Mr Frank A Spencer, who succeeded Mr Moore in 1943, devoted the seventeen years of his headmastership to developing the school and winning recognition for its status. A milestone in its history was reached when, in 1957, Mr Spencer was elected to the Headmasters' Conference. By the time he retired in 1960 the number of boys had been doubled, whilst friends, Old Boys and parents had banded together with a will to raise money for a new wing with five additional form rooms,

boarders, and in 1958 a substantial grant from the Industrial Fund helped to modernise existing science laboratories and build new ones. Mr Spencer and his wife worked unceasingly to keep alive, even with the increased numbers, the intimate family atmosphere which had been born so long ago in the years of exile at Saltburn. Raymond J M Evans, M.A. (Oxon), Ph.D. (London), an Old Silcoatian himself, followed Mr Spencer as Headmaster, and he and his wife also succeeded in preserving that family spirit. Despite her home duties (which included looking after three young children), Mrs Evans, an Oxford Graduate, found time to teach classics and also to supervise the school's domestic staff. Helping to foster that family atmosphere the Silcoates fag system operated in reverse of the usual order: seniors looked after the smaller boys, waiting on them at meal times and helping them, like older brothers. Dr Evans was in turn succeeded by John

Top left: A photograph before lights-out in the school dormitory, Christmas, 1916. *Centre left:* Former Headmaster Mr Sydney Moore pictured with WG Grace. *Left:* A physics class in 1963. *Top right:* Choir practice in 1963. *Above:* Silcoates School was one of the first schools in the area to have computerised banking system which was run by sixth formers, seen here in 1990.

with music, sport, drama and outdoor pursuits featuring strongly.

Baggaley who was Headmaster for 13 years before retirement in 1991. He was educated at Queen Elizabeth Grammar School in Wakefield, and Keble College, Oxford where he gained an Oxford Blue in Rugby. His wife Sara was also an Oxford graduate and former teacher. In 1991 Paul Spillane, formerly a housemaster at Wellington College and latterly Deputy Head of Trent College, became Headmaster. At the very early stage of his headship the controversial but necessary decision was made to end boarding after 170 years. At the same time the decision was also made to become fully co-

educational. Mr Spillane retired in 2008 after 17 years at the helm and the school gave a warm welcome to its new Headmaster, Darryl Wideman, M.A. (Oxon), previously Deputy Headmaster at Ratcliffe College in Leicestershire. Despite that long ago fire the school still stands on the outskirts of the villages of Alverthorpe and Wrenthorpe high above the surrounding country and in the midst of 55 acres of lawns and playing fields. Wakefield is conveniently near, yet far enough away for the school to be out of the bustle and noise inevitable in a busy West Riding city. Today there are 540 pupils on the school roll, with an almost equal mix of boys and girls. There are high academic standards, coupled with an appreciation that the development of the all-round character of each child is just as important. Extra-curricular activities flourish,

The school retains its links with what is now the United Reformed Church, though pupils of all denominations and faiths are welcomed and worship is ecumenical in character. Silcoatians, by and large, turn out to be well-rounded individuals who often possess entrepreneurial flare, a willingness to get involved and a common sense approach to life not often found in independent schools.

Perhaps it is the awareness of the school's challenging past that helps its young people today to develop their awareness of how it is possible to achieve success in the face of adversity.

The school has certainly lived up to its motto, Clarior Ex Ignibus – brilliance still flows from the flames.

Top left: *This historic graffiti dating from the Second World War was discovered behind a long-closed shutter door. Would those boys who chalked their names in wartime have imagined we would be reading it in the new millennium?* ***Above left***: *Pupils of Silcoates today.* ***Above***: *Headmaster, Mr Darryl Wideman.* ***Top right and below***: *Silcoates School, 2009.*

Gordon's Tyres - Who is Gordon?

Gordon's Tyres is the largest independent tyre specialist in Yorkshire. The firm offers a full range of garage services from five branches throughout the region to both commercial and private motorists.

The firm has been in business for more than 40 years. But who is Gordon?

In 1953, at the age of just 10, Gordon Wood was already making his way in business collecting scrap metal and selling it on, aided by his brother and using his father's horse and cart.

Gordon saved his earnings and with that money he was able to set up his own business aged just 18. Three years earlier he had left school at the age of 15, wanting to be a mechanic: his father was taking him for an interview at a garage when they crossed paths with an acquaintance, Tom Whitehead, a coal delivery man. Gordon subsequently worked for Tom Whitehead as his apprentice, delivering coal to the Lupset, Kettlethorpe, Lawefield Lane, Darnley and Peacock areas of Wakefield, deferring his hopes of entering the motor trade until later in his life.

As an apprentice Gordon would work Monday to Saturday starting before 7 each morning. He was paid £1 for working on Saturdays and when he asked Tom for a rise he gave him '10 bob' (50p) and promptly sacked him!

By the following Monday, however, Tom had reconsidered, and Gordon was back in work.

Whilst working for Tom Whitehead Gordon passed his driving test and was given more responsibility: soon he was running Tom's business on his own. The work involved lifting hundredweight sacks of coal from the yard single-handed, stacking them on the lorries and then going out delivering them to customers, emptying the sacks into their coal cellars.

Gordon's family had always been supportive of his business ambitions, and mentored by Edwin Newsome, 'a father figure', Gordon was encouraged to set up on his own.

*Above: Gordon Wood, 2009. **Below:** The first Gordon's Tyres on Bradford Road Wrenthorpe, Wakefield.*

Now aged 18 Gordon asked Tom Whitehead if on his retirement he could buy the business. Tom wasn't ready to sell so Gordon bought another coal delivery business from Ernest Waring.

Gordon would pick up coal from either North Gawber or Newmillerdam collieries, getting up at 4.30am, 'knocking up' his lad, Geoff Swift, for work on the way. They would arrive at the colliery weighbridge for 5.30am to collect the first of two coal loads for the day's deliveries.

Over the following 14 years Gordon expanded his coal business to cover rounds in Wrenthorpe, Outwood, Kirkhamgate, East Ardsley and the Leeds areas of Hunslet; Tempest Road and Beeston.

Gordon maintained a growing fleet of delivery vehicles at Wrenthorpe Service Station, Bradford Road, (now Piccadilly Car Garage): it was here that he befriended Tony Lodge who ran the Uniroyal Tyre Unit behind the service station, dealing in vulcanising repairs to tyres.

In the early 1960s Uniroyal relocated to Barnsley and decided not to continue with vulcanising repairs. This left a gap in the market and Gordon decided to set up a second business venture. He bought the now redundant vulcanising equipment from Uniroyal as well as shipping machinery from Canada, asking Tony Lodge to join his business - the first 'Gordon's Tyres' on the Bradford Road, Wrenthorpe, site.

Gordon converted a number of barns on the land, and with the help of his life-long friend, Ken would deal with repairs to tractor and truck tyres.

Geoff Swift would continue delivering the coal that Gordon was still collecting early each morning, though now from Lofthouse colliery. Gordon would also pick up the daily tyre repairs from the likes of ATS/National Tyres/Tyre Services each morning. By the afternoon Gordon and Tony would be busy repairing these tyres ready for return to the customer.

Now Gordon bought a Bradford-based tyre business from David Butterfield, which again included his machinery and a large stock of tyres. By the late 1960s the business was getting busier and busier, so much so that Gordon was employing a staff of five.

In the early 1970s Gordon took the decision to repair car tyres in addition to tractor and truck tyres. After extending the Bradford Road site to its full capacity Gordon decided to remodel the land to provide both purpose-built premises and housing for his growing family.

Gordon demolished the old barns and put in service roads to the new two-level building of Gordon's Tyres. He built four fitting bays in the premises and started running four mobile fitting vans to cater for his growing clientele. He also introduced, and was one of the first to start, seven days a week trading.

Above: The Bradford Road premises after extension in the 1970s. Below: Gordon's Tyres, Castleford.

Having a fleet of company vehicles maintained became increasing problematic, and so Gordon decided to employ mechanics to take on the repair of vehicles - this grew into offering MOTs and servicing for customer cars and vans.

The Bradford Road premises were extended again in the mid-1970s, now with nine bays for fitting and repair as well as purpose-built offices to deal with the ever increasing paperwork. This was a big contrast to the first office, situated in an outbuilding on the site back in the 1960s where Mrs Haigh first began doing the accounts.

According to Mrs Haigh "I remember vividly my interview for the position; for some reason there was a large Stag's head on the windowsill. On my first morning of starting work I arrived to find no one there, later discovering that the mornings were spent delivering and picking up tyres. Undeterred I stayed for a decade and developed a new cash accounting system - previously it had been a bit sporadic."

Gordon expanded the business, buying premises in Horbury, altering them and offering more clients the choice of servicing and car tyre supply and repairs. In 1986 Gordon opened Stanley Gordons Tyres, converting the old cinema on Aberford Road internally but retaining the unique façade of the building.

Here again Gordon applied his winning formula of car repairs and tyres, but also included a parts distribution centre, run by his daughter Rachel

opened in October 2005. A year later the purpose-built Earthmover Tyres (Wakefield) Ltd business was offering supply and repairs nationwide.

Staff numbers have grown dramatically over the last four decades, swelling from five to over 150. Each depot is the responsibility of a dedicated Manager, added to this, all the depots are aided by an experienced Head Office team headed by Administration Manager Pam Stevenson, and more recently by the Group Admin Manager Elaine Frost.

By the late 1980s Gordon had sold the Horbury Depot and concentrated on building the Castleford Gordon's Tyres depot on land purchased some years earlier. This included four car bays and the now usual Gordon's experience: MOT testing, servicing and tyres.

Gordon set up the Leeds Gordon's Tyres in 1994, acquiring two adjacent buildings and knocking them into one large unit initially offering car and truck repairs before also incorporating a new venture, a specialised Earthmover Tyres department. This would become one of the busiest depots due to its geographic location.

At Stocksbridge, a Sheffield Depot was built in 2001. Though this proved to be a nightmare for the builders, it would become a busy and essential asset to the Gordon's Tyres group of companies.

Having outgrown the Bradford Road, Wrenthorpe site, Gordon now bought land at Silkwood Park and built from scratch the easily recognisable Gordon's Tyres Head Office. The site incorporated a car depot, commercial depot, and a new venture, supplying of fork lift truck tyres. The Silkwood Park premises

In the late 1980s Gordon was once again able to call the company a true 'family business' with his wife Margaret having returned to the Administration Team after raising their four daughters, Maxim, Susan, Catherine and Rachel.

Gordon has never deviated from his aspiration to offer good value-for-money tyres and repairs for all manner of vehicles and in the best time possible. He believes strongly in having 'the right people for the right jobs' whether on the shop floor or in the Management Team, but he also maintains that 'a firm hand is needed' to allow the best people to grow with the business.

As for the future, Gordon says that he is never going to retire. He does try and spend more time with his children and grandchildren, as well as ballroom dancing with Margaret. But he also wants to create new successful businesses.

And that's who Gordon is.

Richard Kendall
The Name That Says Property

They say that you can choose your friends, but you can't choose your family.

Well, it's a good job the Kendalls get on with one another as for the past 19 years the members of Richard Kendall's family have worked hand in hand with each other in the family business, Richard Kendall Estate Agent.

Richard Kendall himself has been selling property for the people of Wakefield and the surrounding area for almost 40 years. Richard started working in Estate Agency on 1 November, 1969, at the age of 22 with a firm of Chartered Surveyors and Auctioneers called Laidlaws based at 1, Crown Court, Wakefield, working as a trainee property sales negotiator.

Laidlaws was owned by two partners at the time, Charles Moss and Harry Thornton, specialising in valuations on behalf of financial institutions, commercial estate agency and residential sales. They also had a well known auction room which regularly held two day antique auctions. The manager of the Estate Agency side at that time was Robert (Bob) Abson, and Richard's job was to follow his heels non-stop for the next two years.

In time Bob set up his own Estate Agency business, and Richard was then promoted to Manager of the Residential Department in 1980. Richard enjoyed a pleasant 21 years with the Company, but in the late 1980s, at a time when Building Societies and other financial institutions were purchasing Estate Agencies to try and enhance their mortgage book, Abbey National Building Society purchased Laidlaws and turned the name into 'Cornerstone'.

At the same time the TSB Bank, who wanted to open a network of Estate Agencies within Yorkshire, were looking to recruit. With the arrival of Cornerstone at Laidlaws, Richard didn't quite see eye to eye with the new establishment and took the opportunity to work for the TSB. He was appointed Yorkshire Operation Manager, opening their flagship branch in Northgate in 1990. Unfortunately the position was not long lived and the recession of the early 1990s came, and along with it, in July 1991, came the downfall of the TSB Home Centre.

After considering various options Richard decided it was time to open up his own Estate Agency. Having already spent over 20 years in Estate Agency, it was what he knew and what he was certainly good at. On 1 October, 1991, Richard Kendall Estate Agent open their first office, situated at 49 Northgate in Wakefield. The premises were formally Needhams Estate Agency and Insurance Brokers with a stock of 23 houses. Richard paid £1,000 for the business with one of the properties on the books belonging to the previous owner. It was in fact his first sale, and completion took place the week before Christmas; not a bad return on an initial investment after only just over 2 months.

When Richard took over the business there was no lettings department, and the main focus was solely on the sale of residential properties, and in any event the rental market was not in full swing.

However, Richard still recalls one particular day when a member of the public called into the office and asked if he had any rented properties available and the answer was, of course, that he did not. Then a second person came in and asked the question, and again the answer was the same, although when a third person walked through the door with the same question, all in the same day, the answer was "yes, we do deal in rented property, but we haven't any available at this moment in time". Straight away Richard started to advertise the fact that the firm dealt in rented accommodation and for the first few months he ran this department alongside house sales.

At that time Richard's wife Jennifer was working with a firm of Civil Engineers in Wakefield. The Company announced that it was closing down its operation in Wakefield and of course this meant that Jennifer was made redundant.

As unemployment figures were then nearing the levels that we are experiencing today, Jennifer informed Richard that she had come to a decision to come on board and run the newly formed Rented Department at Richard Kendall Estate Agent. Jennifer was no stranger to the commercial world, as she had spent the majority of her career in property, firstly as a legal secretary and also secretary to the Clerk and Chief Financial Officer of the then Wakefield Rural District Council. Furthermore, she had previously worked as a lettings officer for Wakefield

Metropolitan District Council, and also dealt with a private portfolio of rented properties for family members.

It was obvious that she should join the firm and start up the Rented Department. The office at Northgate measured just 18 feet by 12, so there was little room for both a husband and wife team to work together in it. The decision was made that she would operate the Rented Department from the family home in Horbury, in their spare bedroom.

Over the next twelve months instructions on rented properties steadily grew, so much so that Richard and Jennifer invited Elizabeth Kirk to join the firm, also working from the family home. Elizabeth, who is now a Director of the company, has been in property nearly all her working life; she would be a strong ally of Jennifer's in helping her grow the Rented Department.

However, working this way didn't come without its issues and before long the decision to move to new premises was made. As luck would have it the firm was very fortunate that an Estate Agent located nearby in Horbury had decided to close down. Richard knew the landlord of the premises very well; he was in fact Richard's old boss at Laidlaws where he had previously worked for 21 years. Richard was able to obtain the keys there and then: he opened for business three days later at 4, Cluntergate, Horbury. The firm has also since acquired the

Top left: Founder, Richard Kendall. Left: The first Richard Kendall Estate Agents at 49, Northgate, Wakefield. Above, left to right: Nicola Smithson, Richard Schora and Nikki Steel, pictured in 1992.

www.richardkendall.co.uk

adjoining premises at 2, Cluntergate, which has double the size of the office to accommodate the growth of the rental department.

Since then Jennifer and Elizabeth have taken the rental department from strength to strength. The department now deals with over 1,000 lettings every year, on top of the properties that it also manages on behalf of clients. The lettings team totals eight people, plus a dedicated accountant, making this department not only one of the largest in the area, but also one of the most efficient.

The sales department also proved to be going from strength to strength which gave rise to the need for alternative accommodation for the Estate Agency, and in 1994 Richard secured premises just across the road at 66, Northgate, at about the same time that Simon Kendall joined the firm.

Following training at Wakefield Catering College, Simon had travelled south to work in the kitchens of a Country House Hotel called Bishopstrow House, in Warminster, under the Head Chef of the Year 1990, Christopher Suitor. However, the close working environment, long working hours and highly stressful working conditions, gave cause for Simon to leave the kitchens at the ripe old age of 18 and joined the family firm.

Simon began his Estate Agency career working in the back offices, sticking photographs on brochures and photocopying, before being given the opportunity to go out with the members of the Valuation department to learn the fundamental facts of

valuing residential properties. It wasn't long before he became a fully fledged Residential Valuer working along side the 5-strong team. This gave Richard the confidence to stop valuing himself and concentrate on running the company from within the office. Now, Simon is fully in charge of the Valuation Department, together with two experienced Valuers, and a trainee Valuer. The successful department is currently obtaining around 60% of the market share of all the properties that come to the market in Wakefield, which is an excellent effort in today's conditions.

Four years on and the time came again to expand the business. On the back of the success of the Horbury office Richard decided to open another sales office in Ossett. The original plan was to open offices in Bank Street, however, a good friend who was also one of Richard's long terms clients intervened; Malcolm Asquith, informed him that his accountants needed to relocate from Station Road, therefore, the decision was made and the Ossett office opened here in October 1998.

The last office to open under the Richard Kendall banner was Normanton. Richard had been informed that an Estate Agency wanted to close down at 21, Market Place, one Monday morning. At lunchtime Richard went to see the Landlord and after coming to a satisfactory arrangement, was fully operational that afternoon. That was in April 2005, and has been a great success story ever since, as with the other 3 offices.

The last of the family to join the business was Claire. After a spell at Northumbria University studying Property Surveying, in 1999 Claire travelled to London to start her training as a Chartered

four fully qualified Domestic Energy Assessors to carry out this work.

In the 40 years that Richard has been working in the residential housing market of Wakefield he has seen many changes. At its peak, Richard has employed over 60 staff. He started his own business with just 23 properties to now selling over 1,000 homes each year. The rental department manages over 700 properties and finds tenants for hundreds more landlords. Over the years Richard has also formed Mortgage Solutions and each of the departments of Richard Kendall Estate Agent complements the other, making it the leading Estate Agency in the Wakefield

Surveyor. After qualifying 2 years later as a Member of the Royal Institution of Chartered Surveyors, Claire stayed in London for another five years before relocating to the Leeds office of the firm she worked for. However, after only 8 months back in Yorkshire Claire soon realised that she would rather be working with her family and followed in her brother's footsteps and joined the family firm in February, 2007. Needless to say, the family was delighted and Claire has firmly found her feet, taking the Company from strength to strength.

In late 2007, with the introduction of Home Information Packs, Richard Kendall Estate Agent formed a new Company within the Estate Agency named 'EnergySmart'. The sole purpose of the Company was to produce Energy Performance Certificates, which are a mandatory part of HIPs, and the Company now has

area. Today, Richard has a number of long serving members of staff with 7 having been with the firm for over 10 years and another 5 not far off this milestone.

So what of the next 20 years of Richard Kendall Estate Agent? Well one thing is for certain Richard Kendall Estate Agent will continue to be a family run business providing a guaranteed personal service.

Top left: A staff Christmas weekend away to Barcelona, one of many weekends arranged by Richard to European destinations. Above: Richard, Jennifer, Claire and Simon Kendall. Below: The Richard Kendall Wakefield premises today.

Asquith Homes - Quality Building for Over 50 Years

The most valuable thing most of us possess is our home. Yet we seldom ask who built the house we live in. In the last half century, however, one local builder has done more than any other to provide quality homes for local people.

Mention the name of Asquith to people around Wakefield and the chances are that they will instantly recognise it. If they are from Ossett they may even live in an Asquith home - the family-run company has been responsible for building a large proportion of the town over the last 50 years.

From building one or two houses to crafting a whole neighbourhood, the company's philosophy of building stylish, comfortable, homes that last, has served it and its clients very well indeed.

Today Asquith's has one of the finest reputations in the area, and it is dedicated to carrying on a family tradition of house building

The company has come a long way since its humble beginnings in a small first floor room on Teall Street, Ossett. Company founder John Asquith, known to all as Jack, started out making wooden children's toys and bespoke carpentry goods.

Moving to larger premises at the end of Teall Street, Jack subsequently specialised in the production of coffins. He became a well respected local undertaker. Production soon diversified, however, into the supply of joinery products for the construction industry. Employing a significant number of carpenters even at this stage, the firm would become one of the main contractors in the district for the supply and installation of joinery goods for the likes of Evans of Leeds and the local councils.

Close to the premises in Teall Street, Jack built a bungalow where he lived with his wife, son and his two daughters, Margaret and Wendy. The site had originally been the children's old nursery school.

It was in 1962, when still aged just 23, that the eldest of Jack's children, John Malcolm Asquith, always known as Malcolm, became convinced that the company could become a house builder itself rather than simply supply the industry with joinery products.

Top left: Malcolm Asquith, founder of Asquith Homes. **Above:** Asquith Homes' 25 Bank Street premises. **Below:** A prestigious Asquith housing project, Elder Mews. These were built adjacent to the bungalow in Teall Street, which can just be seen bottom left, built by the company.

Always keen on football, Malcolm Asquith was an avid Huddersfield Town fan, never missing a game. His passion and devotion was such that he was instrumental in the development of the new McAlpine Stadium at Huddersfield as a Director of Kirklees Stadium Development Ltd 1993-99. He served as a Director of Huddersfield Town F.C. from 1992 to 1999 and became Vice Chairman of the Club in 1995 and was Chairman from 1997 to 1999.

When the club was in dire financial trouble Malcolm helped - along with existing directors - to bring about an upsurge in fortunes in the next few years as the club moved from Leeds Road to its new stadium. He later was awarded the position of Life Vice-President of Huddersfield Town F.C. He was also consistently involved with charity work through Ossett 41 Club and Rotary, of which he was President twice in 1989-90 and 1998-99.

That year, inspired by Malcolm Asquith's vision, a new limited company was set up, J & J.M. Asquith (Joiners & Builders) Ltd, and the new company set about building its first ever house.

Having attended Ossett Grammar School between 1949 to 1954 Malcolm had gone on to Leeds College of Building gaining his ONC and HNC between 1954 and 1959.

Working as a carpenter from a young age, Malcolm possessed an exceptional talent for business. However, his abilities were not limited solely to the construction industry. Malcolm was also a skilled footballer, known for his speed and goal scoring ability. For years he held several records for athletics at his school. A speedy right winger, Malcolm later played soccer for Ossett Common Rovers and Ossett Albion.

Malcolm Asquith was also keenly interested in local politics: at the age of only 32, already a Conservative Councillor, he became Mayor of Ossett Borough Council and was responsible for many improvements to the lives of people living there.

In the meantime, in the 1960s and 1970s, the building company which had been Malcolm's brainchild in 1962 had evolved from its origins building individual houses on single plots. The

business slowly grew to a stage where it was employing 175 workmen and was building on several developments simultaneously. At one stage the company even owned its own coach to provide transport for the staff.

Quality not quantity was a key philosophy. By the late 1970s Malcolm was slowly reducing the company in size, whilst still retaining some of the best craftsmen in Yorkshire. The company is still fortunate to work with these men. Danny Lister, Site Foreman, started

This page: *Other Asquith projects, Vicar Lane (top left), Bank Street (left) and Market Place (above).*

when only 15 years of age under the guidance of Jack and Malcolm. He still works today and has been a key element in maintaining the ongoing quality of the company's housing.

The company moved to new offices in the centre of Ossett at 25, Bank Street in late 1999 and rented its old workshops.

The site of Asquith's old office, yard and joinery workshops at Teall Street has now become Elder Mews, a prestigious Asquith housing project, which began in 2006. Building work on the select development of only 21 homes comprising 14 townhouses and 7 high specification apartments at Elder Mews was completed in 2008.

Sadly, Malcolm Asquith passed away in April 2008 aged 69 years but not before he had touched the hearts of so many people, not just locally but worldwide. A true Yorkshireman he was well liked by all he met and was known for his upbeat attitude to life, generosity and infectious sense of humour. He certainly left his mark on Ossett and all other aspects of life he was involved with.

Pictures: *Windsor Court (Top), Barclays, Bank Street (left), Mallin House, Sanford Court (below).*

Moving premises was to prove very beneficial. The company had always marketed the majority of developments itself from show houses on site, though with the occasional help from local estate agents. Relocation meant sole marketing of Asquith's homes for sale and rental by the company itself. This hands-on marketing was a preferable method, and customers appreciated dealing with the builders direct. The majority of Asquith homes rent and sell by recommendation from previous customers, something which the firm is very proud of.

Asquith's continues to be noted for its high quality affordable homes in the right locations, whether for sale or rental. That reputation continues with the next generation as Malcolm's sons take the business forward.

Projects currently in the pipeline include 'Elevation' at Alverthorpe, an ultra modern development of 43 high specification, two bedroom en-suite apartments set within a secure gated community. Nearly all the apartments have large balconies and the scheme includes a feature lift as well as communal landscaped grounds with decked areas overlooking Alverthorpe Beck.

At Valley Road, Ossett the company is working on a small development of 3/4 bedroom townhouses on generous private garden plots with good aspects close to the centre of Ossett.

Old Bank Road/York Road is yet another location earmarked for development by Asquiths. The site comprises two separate developments. The first involves conversion of an existing three storey stone mill building into 20 apartments with its own entrance, parking and cycle store. Adjacent to the mill development will be around 40 newly built dwellings mainly of townhouses with some apartments and separate private entrance. Around two acres in total, the site has pleasant aspects with playing fields to the rear and well kept allotments to the front. There is also provision for generous amenity space within the development.

As for commercial property, Asquith's is also keen to develop the Seemore Shopping Centre, Seemore Arcade and the former Cock & Bottle site which will be redeveloped into an indoor market with much needed public toilet facilities and town centre apartments. Northfield Mill on Church Street is currently being converted back to its former glory by conversion into private affordable split level apartments.

Asquith Homes are now focusing their energies into the regeneration of Ossett Town centre. The company is applying for planning permission to develop the now dated parade of shops

on Dale Street in Ossett. The scheme incorporates a two storey extension to the existing flat roof to provide 11 low cost rental apartments - the type of property which is in short supply in the area.

The appearance of the existing building will be brought up to date whilst still complementing the Town Hall and the rebuilt Co-operative opposite. Regeneration is long overdue for the parade: the project is effectively a public scheme but with private funding.

Today Malcolm Asquith's sons, Jonathan and Matthew, having benefited from the guidance provided by their father, are committed to taking the family business forward with no compromise on quality and the values the company has stood by for over 50 years.

Top left: The former Cock & Bottle site. Above: Seemore Shopping Centre. Left: Northfield Mill on Church Street. Below: Jonathan Asquith (right) and Matthew Asquith. Jonathan has worked on the development sites since leaving school and Matthew joined the company after qualifying in International Law to Masters level and working in London for a few years.

Brotherton Esseco Ltd - Over 130 Years and Still Growing

Brotherton Esseco Ltd was founded in 1878, as a small ammonia distilling works and today still operates from its original site in Calder Vale Road, Wakefield. From its earliest beginnings the company specialised in the manufacture of ammonia salts. Over the years the product range has been broadened, whilst at the same time maintaining a key position in ammonia salts. The company is a major supplier to both the domestic and international markets.

The current product range revolves around the use of several key raw materials including Sulphur Dioxide, Carbon Dioxide, Ammonia, Alkali Hydroxides and several key organic acids.

The Brothertons were a Manchester family involved in the textile trade and Edward, the eldest of six children, was born in 1856, the year in which the Crimean War came to an end. He noted that many chemical manufacturers were pouring away a fortune in ammonia by-products.

Relatives of the Brotherton family, the Dysons from Wakefield, agreed to back Edward to the tune of £3,000. A new chemical company, the first in Wakefield, was opened under the name Dyson Sons and Brotherton on 1 September, 1878. Edward Brotherton was just 22 years old.

He lived on the site for the first five years, getting up and out into the factory well before the arrival of the morning shift. In 1893 he secured a contract from Birmingham Corporation for gas liquor and spent iron oxide. A year later, the Brotherton Birmingham plant was nearing production when, at the Society of Chemical Industry dinner in Edinburgh, Edward met up with George Bielby, a businessman who had sold his process for manufacturing cyanide, which used large quantities of ammonia, to the Cassel company.

Edward was engaged to supply ammonia liquor to the Cassel company, a relationship that eventually made Edward Brotherton firstly an important shareholder in Cassel's, afterwards deputy chairman and, on the death of George Bielby in 1927, chairman.

Brotherton and Company now began to expand in earnest as coal tar products were added to the firm's growing list of products. But the first chemical works at Calder Vale Road had not been forgotten in the expansion. New products required a forest of tall chimneys that dominated the skyline. Meanwhile Edward, even with his numerous business

Top left: Founder, Lord Brotherton. *Left:* The Calder Vale factory in the 1930s. *Inset left:* A Thorneycroft Brotherton lorry in the 1940s. *Above:* Staff enjoying a celebratory drink in the early 1960s.

E.A Brotherton gave each of his workers a gold sovereign for every year of service. A quote from Sir Edward to a Yorkshire Evening News reporter, highlighted his work ethic when he said, " Unsparing effort is the whole secret of success in industry and business".

Lord Brotherton died in 1930 after a long illness at Kirkham Abbey. Among his many benefactions was a gift of the magnificent new library at Leeds University. The library was built at a cost of £120,000 and opened on 6 October, 1936, by the Archbishop of Canterbury.

interests across the north, was active in Wakefield's social and political life.

In 1902 Edward Brotherton became Mayor of Wakefield, the same year winning a seat in Parliament. He continued to represent Wakefield's interests for eight years. One of his public-spirited ideas to encourage thrift amongst children led to savings books, each with an initial credit of one shilling, being given to 60,000 school children. After the first world war Edward had a special medal designed and presented it, along with a small amount of money, to soldiers who had suffered as prisoners of war. His spiralling fortune brought Edward great pleasure as he assumed the role of city benefactor, but his personal life was marred by tragedy. Edward had married at the age of 27 just when he was beginning to expand his chemical empire. Sadly, just a year later his young wife died in childbirth. He never married again, choosing instead to lavish his affections on his nephews and nieces, and spending his money on his sister's children's education, the eldest of whom Charles Ratcliffe, was Edward's chosen successor at Brotherton and Company.

Charles Ratcliffe joined the company in 1904 and in return Charles took his uncle's name and later, on Edward's death, his place as chairman of Brotherton and Company. Charles Brotherton showed the same generous nature as his uncle, creating his own Charles Brotherton Trust with a handsome donation of £250,000, the yearly income from which is still distributed amongst the cities and towns that have been associated with Brotherton and Company.

In 1928, two years before his death, Edward Allen Brotherton was elevated to the Peerage and turned to his adopted city for his title, becoming Lord Brotherton of Wakefield. In the same year, to mark the Company's Jubilee Anniversary, Colonel Sir

In 2007 guests from as far afield as France, New Zealand and Luxembourg gathered to commemorate the 150th anniversary of Leeds University's greatest benefactor. There was an equally prominent Wakefield connection, as around 35 proud relatives joined a special reception at the Brotherton Library to celebrate the life and achievements of Lord Brotherton of Wakefield (1856–1930). Among the guests was Dr Roger Perry, Managing Director of Brotherton Esseco Ltd, which is today a wholly-owned subsidiary of the Esseco Group based in Trecate, Italy.

The former activities of Esseco UK LLP were fully integrated into the business of Brotherton's on 1 January, 2009.

Top left: Views in and around Calder Vale works.
Above: Dr Roger Perry (centre) is pictured here with Lord Brotherton's great nephew Christopher Brotherton Ratcliffe (left) and great nephew David Brotherton (right), both direct decendants of Lord Brotherton's sister, Florence.
Left: A bird's eye view of Brotherton Esseco Ltd, 2009.

Warburtons - Using Their Loaf

Warburtons is Britain's favourite family baker. The company has enjoyed a close relationship with Wakefield for more than 20 years, and with Yorkshire for even longer.

The Warburtons story began in 1876 when Thomas Warburton and his wife Ellen opened a small grocery shop in Bolton, Lancashire, with help from Thomas' brother George. From these humble beginnings – not least Ellen Warburton's famed loaves and flour cakes - the business would grow become the country's leading independent baker.

George's son Henry joined the business aged just 16. By the age of 25 he was a Master Baker and was in charge. Between the late 1880s and 1915 Warburtons expanded, moving bakeries four times.

Henry Warburton died in 1936, leaving the business to his three sons - George, Harry and Billy. During the late 1940s, Warburtons' expansion continued. In the 1950s there was a realisation that a strong team of good people to help the family build the business was also a vital ingredient of success. The decade saw senior personnel from outside the family joining the business.

Warburtons grew through acquisition of several smaller companies in the North West, including Imperial Bakeries, manufacturers of Soreen Malt Loaf - still a market-leading brand today. Between 1951 and 1965, Warburtons group bread sales doubled through its five bakeries and 38 confectionery shops.

The company continued to thrive into the 1970s, consolidating the great advances of the previous two decades and building new bakeries.

Warburtons' relationship with the Yorkshire region began in the early 1970s with the opening of a distribution depot in Leeds. In

1985, the baker opened its first production facility in Yorkshire at Westgate End bakery in Wakefield. At that time, Warburtons employed 250 people at Westgate End, baking over 700,000 loaves per week. Over the ensuing years, the Warburtons brand grew ever more popular, and with growing demand, the company began exploring new sites within Wakefield which

Top left: *Rachel Warburton outside their first shop in Bolton.* ***Below:*** *The Warburtons family outside the bakery with delivery vans and drivers.* ***Above:*** *Nellie Wallace the music hall star tasting the Eatmore Malt loaf in the 1930s with Henry Warburton, his wife Rachel (left) and son George (right).*

Howden in East Yorkshire and at Premier Park.

The Howden depot covers 15,000 sq ft. and was opened in July 2008, replacing the old distribution depot in Gilberdyke, while Premier Park sits in Oulton, Leeds, and together created a distribution network ensuring Warburtons can deliver fresh bread across the region every day.

In 2009, Warburtons' Executive Director Brett Warburton welcomed Secretary of State For Education Ed Balls to the opening of a brand new learning centre at Tuscany Park named the W.H.E.A.T Centre (Warburtons Help Education and Training). This was a first for Warburtons in Yorkshire, providing its employees with the essential tools and resources to build upon their key skills in English, Maths and IT.

would allow it to increase its production capacity, employ more local people and cement its place in the fabric of Wakefield.

Warburtons found its new home on the outskirts of the city and in 2006, moved to the purpose-built, state-of-the-art bakery at Tuscany Park. This, Warburtons largest bakery, boasts a state-of-the-art visitor centre, which tells the story of bread making and the history of Warburtons.

A £60 million investment, Warburtons Tuscany Park bakery covers 12.9 acres and produces 131 million loaves of bread and 40 million packets of sandwich rolls every single year. Standing end-to-end, the products baked at Tuscany Park every week would stretch from Wakefield to New York!

The new bakery, Warburtons twelfth, and the largest in Europe, created an additional 200 jobs and quadrupled bread production in Yorkshire.

In addition to Tuscany Park, Warburtons also has local depots at

Warburtons has expanded its market into southern England from its traditional heartland in the North, and has ambitious plans to continue development of the Warburtons brand. In 2009, the family baker was the first to take advantage of a change in the law to begin providing customers with a 600g loaf, meeting a growing demand from those who found a small loaf did not go far enough in their families while larger loaves often went to waste.

In its long history in Yorkshire, Warburtons the family baker has been a regular supporter of local charities and community groups. From sports kit donations to local junior football teams to bread donations to the local hospice, Warburtons is a proud community partner in Wakefield.

Top left: A shopper in the 1950s buying her Warburtons' Eatmore loaf. **Bottom left:** *Work begins on building Warburtons' Tuscany Park bakery.* **Left and below:** *Interior and exterior views of the completed state-of-the-art Tuscany Park bakery.*

E.M.D Parkinson Ltd - First Choice for the Last Service

As the old saying goes – only two things are certain in life: death and taxes. Though in fact taxes can be avoided, death is an absolute. At such times help for bereaved families in coping with the practical difficulties they face is more than welcome. And the best source of help is a professional undertaker.

In times gone by the business of undertaking was often a part time activity. Often a neighbour who also doubled as a midwife would take charge of 'laying out'. Frequently the task of organising a funeral would be a sideline for a local joiner who would make coffins in addition to his more usual business of making shelves or door frames.

In the course of the 20th century, however, the business of undertaking became increasingly specialist. And with that increasing specialisation has come ever greater professionalism.

Without doubt one of the most professional and experienced firms of local undertakers is E.M.D Parkinson Ltd.

Funeral Directors E.M.D Parkinson Ltd was founded by Edward M.D Parkinson just after the start of the 20th century. Originally the firm dealt in horses and trading, mainly as Carriage Masters.

Edward Parkinson provided horses and carriages (including hearses) for anyone who required them. The

Company became Registered in 1923 and at the same time became involved with haulage, as well as setting up in business as a coal merchant.

It wasn't until 1930 that Edward Parkinson decided to become established as a Funeral Director. This decision came about when he realised that he was supplying all the requirements for Funeral Directing to other people. His was the first company in Wakefield to be able to offer fully inclusive funerals as all the equipment was at hand.

Top left: Founder, Edward M.D Parkinson.
Left: An early photograph of Austin Parkinson, son of the founder, when the company was involved in haulage and coal merchanting.
Above: Jack Thorpe who joined the company in 1947 pictured alongside a Ford lorry from the company's haulage days.

The horses, hearses and funeral parlour were all based at 14, Arundel Street. All other undertakers were at that time having to hire different people for different aspects of the job.

Austin Parkinson, Edward's son, joined the company in 1935 and a year later he was sent to Canada and America to further his knowledge of undertaking and to broaden his outlook in the latest developments in funeral directing by 'morticians', as the Americans would say.

After the second world war Austin took control of the funeral directing side and this gradually took over all other aspects of the business until eventually they were dropped.

One of the biggest changes down the years was the virtual disappearance of horses. By the middle of the 20th century the horse-drawn hearse was a rarity, long-since replaced by the motor hearse. Edward Parkinson, however, kept his love for horses right until his death in 1958.

The business continued to thrive, moving first to a former residence for nuns, St Gabriel's House, in Laburnum Road, before settling in its present address in the centre of town at The White House, in Lower York Street, Wakefield.

Looking after the funeral side since Austin Parkinson's retirement in 1990 is Andrew Smith, who now carries on the

There is a full 24-hour personal service so that someone is always able to give free help and advice with enquiries and instructions.

The Company of E.M.D Parkinson has been in the heart of Wakefield since the turn of the last century. Today the firm hopes to continue serving the community for many years yet to come. Although much has altered down the years some things

remain unchanged: not least the level of care, consideration and courtesy which has been a hallmark of the firm since its earliest days.

Top right: Horse drawn hearses were the only method of transportation in the 1930s when motorisation became commonplace. Left: Early advertising for E.M.D. Parkinson on Chantry Bridge around 1915. Above: Austin Parkinson pictured in 1995. Below: Two views of E.M.D Parkinson's premises, The White House, Lower York Street, Wakefield.

tradition of good professional service, whilst being sympathetic and helpful at a time of great distress to the bereaved. The company today is a member of The Society of Allied and Independent Funeral Directors and offers everything anyone could need for a funeral service. Although most funerals the firm undertakes still follow a traditional pattern, Parkinson's has the experience and resources to cater for any individual wishes. There is a Private Chapel of Rest and the firm can assist in arranging anything from pre-paid funerals to horse drawn hearses.

William Lamb Footwear

At the Forefront of Design, While Maintaining the Highest Standards of Production

William Lamb Footwear Ltd, based in Bottom Boat Road, Stanley, Wakefield, is a privately owned business that has grown since 1887 to become the United Kingdom's leading footwear distributor. It's a position the firm has achieved by being at the forefront of design, while maintaining the highest standards of production.

The company manufactures footwear for the world's largest retailers, with clients including such well known names as Wal-Mart (ASDA), Fred Perry, Tesco, Clarkes and Start-rite. In addition to the UK market William Lamb shoes are also sold in the USA, Sweden, Denmark, Germany, France, Hong Kong and Japan. Key brands are Gluv, Buckle My Shoe and Fred Perry. The firm also produces Disney, Spiderman and many other children's brands under licence.

The business was founded in 1887 by William Lamb, the present Chairman's grandfather.

William Lamb had previously been a coal miner before taking the step of setting himself up in business making the clogs then worn in the coal mines and mills of the West Riding.

Leather and wooden clog soles were made locally for many decades. When eventually larger scale manufacturing took place materials were sourced from the UK and other European countries, notably Italy.

Clogs were not the only early product. During the first world war the firm produced army boots; and when the second world war broke out production of army boots was resumed alongside the production of gas mask cases.

In 1920, in partnership with a local rhubarb grower, William Lamb also owned a cinema in Stanley (now a Gordon's car tyre depot) – inevitably it was referred to locally as 'The Clog & Rhubarb Picture House'.

Company founder William Lamb (senior) was succeeded in 1923 by his son, William Lamb (junior) - the present Chairman's father. He began to diversify production into

boots as well as clogs. Subsequently Ruth Lamb (Mrs William Lamb junior) became Chairman, followed by her son, the late David Lamb.

David Lamb joined the firm in 1960. The company now became one of the first to use a novel construction technique for vulcanising the upper part of the shoe to the sole. As a consequence production at that time became focused on football boots.

The current Chairman of the group is Stuart Lamb, who joined the firm in 1966. He is now the third generation of his family to bear the nickname 'Clogger' Lamb.

In 1967 William Lamb were one of the first UK footwear businesses to begin manufacturing trainers, which proved very popular, and 2 further manufacturing sites were added at Ouzlewell Green and South Kirby. During this manufacturing expansion in the 1970s the firm grew from employing just 35 staff to

over 800 in three factories. Today all manufacturing is done overseas. Some 85 staff are still employed in Wakefield, however, and a further 100 at overseas offices.

The overseas business began in 1983 when Gola Sports was acquired, and importing from the Far East and Italy began. In 2000 all Lamb's European manufacturing ceased.

The company's main office and large warehouse are still in Stanley, but the company also has offices in Thailand, Vietnam, China and India to control production in those countries. The firm's strong manufacturing heritage ensures detailed control of the whole manufacturing process, from design to delivery wherever that might be in the world.

Most categories of footwear are produced although there is a strong bias towards children's shoes.

William Lamb Footwear Ltd has been producing high quality footwear since the reign of Queen Victoria. It remains committed to providing exceptional value through innovative design and customer service

The firm has one of the largest teams of shoe designers in the UK with very strong support from its highly experienced technicians The design department has 20 full-time staff and produces more than 500 new designs a month - over 6,000 a year. Some 1,000 styles may be in production at any time.

Annual sales are now in excess of £40 million, a sum which represents almost eight million pairs of shoes. Due to improvements in technology and overseas production the sale prices to the customer have remained steady whilst the volume of sales has expanded hugely.

William 'Clogger' Lamb would have surely been astonished.

Far left and above left: William Lamb clog makers and the WM Lamb warehouse in the early days. **Left:** *Stuart Lamb, current Chairman of William Lamb Footwear Ltd.*

Crofton High School - Achieving Together

The new building was a major advance in the educational facilities in the area - not surprising since it had cost over £250,000. At that time there were 378 pupils with 17 teaching staff.

In September 1974, after local re-organisation, the school became Crofton High School, now with some 700 pupils and a teaching staff of over 40.

Crofton High School located in the High Street, Crofton, is not only one of the best-equipped schools in the Wakefield area but also one of the most well-regarded.

It was founded in the 1950s as Crofton Secondary School to take pupils from Crofton, Walton and Sharlston.

In 1964 the school moved to brand new accommodation capable of housing 540 pupils, bringing to a close ten years of temporary accommodation in Crofton Old Hall. The architects of the new building were Messrs JGL Poulson in collaboration with the County Architect's Department.

On Saturday 17 July, 1965, the school was officially opened by County Alderman Mrs J Smith JP.

Pupil numbers continued to rise throughout the second half of the 1970s, and by 1980 over 1,000 attended the school. To meet the increase in numbers new buildings were added: Mangnall in 1974, Waterton in 1979 and Harrison in 1984.

By the early 1990s an annual intake of about 200 became the established norm.

In August 1995 the school suffered a major fire caused by an electrical fault. The whole of the main school was totally destroyed. Although the outlying buildings were saved, the fire left the school community facing some three years in temporary accommodation. Crofton Old Hall was again pressed into service and 21 temporary classrooms were constructed on site. It is worthy of note that although there

Top left and left: *Views of Crofton High School prior to the fire in 1995.* ***Above:*** *The devastating effects the fire had on the school can be seen in these two photographs.*

were only four weeks between the fire and a new term starting the following September, not a day of pupil learning was lost.

Messages of support, still kept securely at school, were received from within the community and throughout Wakefield. Letters were received from residents of Crofton who had heard about the fire whilst away on holiday who they took time out of their break to write to Mr Myers, the headteacher.

The fire devastated all those connected to the school. Information still contained in the archive shows diary entries and letters from pupils – one in particularly refers to the demolition of the chimney and the sadness she felt that she would no longer see the chimney again.

A new school, designed to accommodate an increase in student numbers, was built on the footprint of the old building. Some aspects were totally re-positioned, however, including the school's main reception area which is now situated at the front of the school off High Street.

Adaptations to the existing buildings were made to provide additional floor area to Waterton and Mangnall, and the first floor of Harrison Building was altered to allow for additional science accommodation.

Main contract works to the value of £3.66 million began in February 1997 and were completed on 23 February, 1998. All remaining work, adaptations and external work were completed on 28 May that year.

The new school was officially opened on Friday 9 October, 1998, by then Chair of the Governing Body, Graham P Jackson OBE BEM JP.

To commemorate the opening of the new school a Time Capsule was mounted in a glass case in the library at the school, containing memorabilia from that year.

In 2005 Mr Myers retired after 15 years at the helm to be followed by a new Head, Jez Horsley.

That same year the school was granted Specialist Status in Maths and Computing.

Today the school is a vibrant place boasting some of the best academic achievements, pupil attendance and behaviour rates in Wakefield. It no longer primarily takes pupils from the three villages of Crofton, Walton and Sharlston, but now takes pupils from across Wakefield including Normanton, Ryhill, Havercroft, South Hiendley and Hemsworth.

There is still an annual intake of 200, with an overall student population of around 1,000.

Examination results are outstanding. The school has twice received national recognition from the Specialists Schools and Academies Trust (SSAT), establishing Crofton High School not only as one of most successful secondary schools in the County but also in England.

*Above pictures: Pupils at work. **Below:** An aerial view of Crofton High School, 2009.*

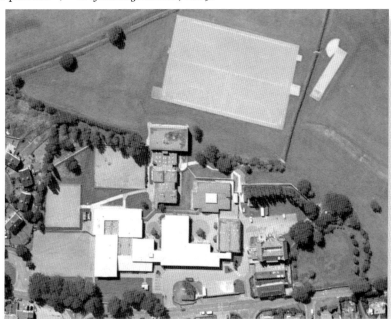

H.Hofmann & Sons Ltd - Champion Pies & Sausage

For over a century 'Hofmann's' and 'pork pies' have been synonymous. The firm's famous pork pies have won many championship awards. John and Nigel Hofmann even took some of their award-winning pies and black puddings to 10 Downing Street and presented them to the Prime Minister.

Hofmann's pork pies have also been presented to the Houses of Parliament after the Wakefield firm won the Great Yorkshire Pork Pie Championship.

Each Christmas the firm sells tens of thousands of its famous pies, with customers queuing down the street for a warm pie fresh from the ovens as early as 6 am.

But pork pies are not the only product made by H.Hofmann

& Sons Ltd. The firm's pork sausages have been crowned champions three years in a row. Traditional quality in everything is the key. Fresh pork legs, for example, are cured into hams in exactly the same way that the present proprietors' grandfather used to cure them. Meat is sourced from local farms, with a relationship built up, in many cases, over many decades and down the generations.

The Hofmann family first arrived in Wakefield in 1896 after leaving Halle, a village near Stuttgart, along with the

Top: Charles Hofmann outside his Westgate shop in the 1930s. Left: John Hofmann (right) and Nigel Hofmann outside 10 Downing Street with their award-winning black puddings which they presented to the then Prime Minister, John Major.

Frank's sons, Ian and Stephen, would later run the bakers, whilst John's sons, David and Nigel, would take on the butchers and pie business. John's wife, Betty, ran the pie bakery until 1995. When Frank Hofmann retired in 2004 his sons subsequently left the business. However, the firm now expanded in other directions, running a farm in Sharlston as well as finding new outlets, such as outside catering supplies to pubs and restaurants.

Today bakers start at 2 a.m every day baking fresh bread and cakes. The firm still employs some 60 staff despite ever-increasing automation. All its products are still made from the finest ingredients. Despite a concentration on traditional products plenty of innovation also takes place, with new products being developed such as introducing Wakefield-grown rhubarb to pies and sausages. Testament to the quality can be seen every lunchtime as shoppers queue for a Hofmann's hot pie or hot carvery sandwich. And special orders too are catered for: the firm has even made a three-tier wedding cake out of pork pies.

Traditional products, however, still sell well, such as the thousands of slabs of parkin sold each bonfire night, as well as more traditional wedding cakes made using recipes and decorating skills passed down the generations

Today John Hofmann, now in his eighties, still works every day. David's sons Adam and Robert can often be seen behind the counter in one of the branches whilst Nigel's children Emily and Harry can be found helping on the farm.

Future generations will be able to enjoy Hofmann's pies every bit as much as folk have already been doing for more than a hundred years.

Oesterleins and Zeiglers (all butcher families who settled in Wakefield). Charles Hofmann had been a butcher in Germany and brought with him to Yorkshire the original recipes for sausages, pies and cooked meats.

Charles opened a small shop in Westgate next to the Opera House. Sadly, he died at a relatively early age and his wife, Sophie, kept the business running until their son Harry was old enough to take over.

In 1912 the firm moved to 111 Westgate. At the back was a small yard, garden and a smallholding where they kept chickens, pigs and a few sheep. Above the shop were many large rooms where some of the staff lived. Many staff would stay with the firm for decades: Graham Whitworth, for example, worked for forty years, and Malcolm Spedding. Hofmann's would have no difficulty passing down its prized skills from one generation to the next.

Harry had two sons, John a butcher, and Frank who joined the RAF. After leaving the RAF Frank started the bakery side of the business in Kirkgate opposite the ABC cinema (now the Ridings) whilst John built up the butchery side. Following Harry's death in 1963, the business expanded at Westgate with a pie bakehouse, cake bakehouse and an abattoir. Many of the 50 or so small butchers shops then in Wakefield stocked Hofmann's products

By the 1980s the firm had itself grown to have seven shops. Customers by now also included wholesalers, corner shops, schools, and not least, the supply of pork pies for Wakefield Trinity's home games.

Above left: *Pictured outside the Houses of Paliament are Nigel, Emily and Harry Hofmann with two MP's.* ***Below:*** *David, Nigel and John Hofmann outside the Silver Street shop.*

ACKNOWLEDGMENTS

The publishers would like to sincerely thank a number of individuals and organisations for their help and contribution to this publication.
This book would have been almost impossible without the kind co-operation of the following:

Yorkshire Weekly Newspaper Group Ltd

Wakefield Museum

Wakefield Learning and Local Studies Library

Ossett Library

Bradford Industrial Museum

University of St Andrews, Valentine Collection

The Late Eric L Raper

Mr R G Pearson

Wakefield Trinity Wildcats RLFC

All reasonable steps were taken by the publishers of this book to trace the copyright holders and obtain permission to use the photographs contained herein. However, due to the passage of time certain individuals were untraceable. Should any interested party subsequently come to light, the publishers can be contacted at the phone number printed at the front of this book and the appropriate arrangements will then be made.